Field Guides to Finding a New Career

Accounting, Business, and Finance

The Field Guides to Finding a New Career series

Accounting, Business, and Finance

Advertising, Sales, and Marketing

Arts and Entertainment

Education

Engineering, Mechanics, and Architecture

Film and Television

Food and Culinary Arts

Health Care

Hospitality and Personal Care

Human Services

Information Technology

Internet and Media

Law and Justice

Nonprofits and Government

Outdoor Careers

Public Safety and Law Enforcement

Real Estate

Science

Sports

Travel and Transportation

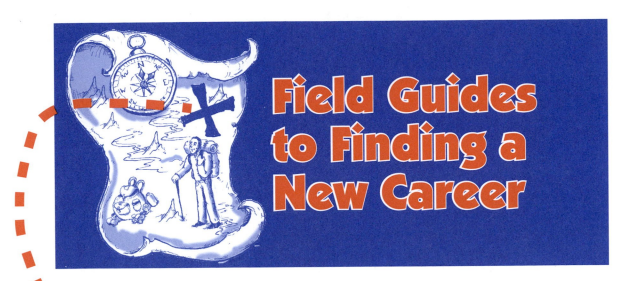

Field Guides to Finding a New Career

Accounting, Business, and Finance

By Candace S. Gulko

Ferguson Publishing
An imprint of Infobase Publishing

Field Guides to Finding a New Career: Accounting, Business, and Finance

Ferguson
An imprint of Infobase Publishing
132 West 31st Street
New York, NY 10001

Library of Congress Cataloging-in-Publication Data

Gulko, Candace S.
Accounting, business, and finance / by Candy Gulko.
    p. cm. — (Field guides to finding a new career)
  Includes bibliographical references and index.
  ISBN-13: 978-0-8160-7994-0 (hardcover : alk. paper)
  ISBN-10: 0-8160-7994-3 (hardcover : alk. paper)
1. Accountants—Juvenile literature.
2. Capitalists and financiers—Juvenile literature.
3. Businesspeople—Juvenile literature. I. Title.
  HF5628.G85 2009
  332.023—dc22

                                                        2009032323

Ferguson books are available at special discounts when purchased in bulk quantities for businesses, associations, institutions, or sales promotions. Please call our Special Sales Department in New York at (212) 967-8800 or (800) 322-8755.

You can find Ferguson on the World Wide Web at http://www.fergpubco.com

Produced by Print Matters, Inc.
Text design by A Good Thing, Inc.
Illustrations by Molly Crabapple
Cover design by Takeshi Takahashi
Cover printed by Bang Printing, Brainerd, MN
Book printed and bound by Bang Printing, Brainerd, MN
Date printed: March 2010

Printed in the United States of America

10 9 8 7 6 5 4 3 2 1

This book is printed on acid-free paper.

Contents

Introduction: Finding a New Career   vii

How to Use This Book   ix

Make the Most of Your Journey   xi

Self-Assessment Quiz   xv

Chapter 1   **Financial Analyst**   **1**

Chapter 2   **Personal Financial Advisor**   **12**

Chapter 3   **Accountant**   **24**

Chapter 4   **Auditor**   **34**

Chapter 5   **Stockbroker**   **44**

Chapter 6   **Brand Manager**   **54**

Chapter 7   **Claims Adjuster**   **63**

Chapter 8   **Bookkeeper**   **73**

Chapter 9   **Insurance Underwriter**   **82**

Chapter 10   **Loan Officer**   **91**

Appendix A   Going Solo: Starting Your Own Business   101

Appendix B   Outfitting Yourself for Career Success   114

Index   125

Introduction: Finding a New Career

Today, changing jobs is an accepted and normal part of life. In fact, according to the Bureau of Labor Statistics, Americans born between 1957 and 1964 held an average of 9.6 jobs from the ages of 18 to 36. The reasons for this are varied: To begin with, people live longer and healthier lives than they did in the past and accordingly have more years of active work life. However, the economy of the twenty-first century is in a state of constant and rapid change, and the workforce of the past does not always meet the needs of the future. Furthermore, fewer and fewer industries provide bonuses such as pensions and retirement health plans, which provide an incentive for staying with the same firm. Other workers experience epiphanies, spiritual growth, or various sorts of personal challenges that lead them to question the paths they have chosen.

Job instability is another prominent factor in the modern workplace. In the last five years, the United States has lost 2.6 *million jobs*; in 2005 alone, 370,000 workers were affected by mass layoffs. Moreover, because of new technology, changing labor markets, ageism, and a host of other factors, many educated, experienced professionals and skilled blue-collar workers have difficulty finding jobs in their former career tracks. Finally—and not just for women—the realities of juggling work and family life, coupled with economic necessity, often force radical revisions of career plans.

No matter how normal or accepted changing careers might be, however, the time of transition can also be a time of anxiety. Faced with the necessity of changing direction in the middle of their journey through life, many find themselves lost. Many career-changers find themselves asking questions such as: Where do I want to go from here? How do I get there? How do I prepare myself for the journey? Thankfully, the Field Guides to Finding a New Career are here to show the way. Using the language and visual style of a travel guide, we show you that reorienting yourself and reapplying your skills and knowledge to a new career is not an uphill slog, but an exciting journey of exploration. No matter whether you are in your twenties or close to retirement age, you can bravely set out to explore new paths and discover new vistas.

Though this series forms an organic whole, each volume is also designed to be a comprehensive, stand-alone, all-in-one guide to getting motivated, getting back on your feet, and getting back to work. We thoroughly discuss common issues such as going back to school, managing your household finances, putting your old skills to work in new situations, and selling yourself to potential employers. Each volume focuses on a broad career field, roughly grouped by Bureau of Labor Statistics' career clusters. Each chapter will focus on a particular career, suggesting new career paths suitable for an individual with that experience and training as well as practical issues involved in seeking and applying for a position.

Many times, the first question career-changers ask is, "Is this new path right for me?" Our self-assessment quiz, coupled with the career compasses at the beginning of each chapter, will help you to match your personal attributes to set you on the right track. Do you possess a storehouse of skilled knowledge? Are you the sort of person who puts others before yourself? Are you methodical and organized? Do you communicate effectively and clearly? Are you good at math? And how do you react to stress? All of these qualities contribute to career success—but they are not equally important in all jobs.

Many career-changers find working for themselves to be more hassle-free and rewarding than working for someone else. However, going at it alone, whether as a self-employed individual or a small-business owner, provides its own special set of challenges. Appendix A, "Going Solo: Starting Your Own Business," is designed to provide answers to many common questions and solutions to everyday problems, from income taxes to accounting to providing health insurance for yourself and your family.

For those who choose to work for someone else, how do you find a job, particularly when you have been out of the labor market for a while? Appendix B, "Outfitting Yourself for Career Success," is designed to answer these questions. It provides not only advice on résumé and self-presentation, but also the latest developments in looking for jobs, such as online resources, headhunters, and placement agencies. Additionally, it recommends how to explain an absence from the workforce to a potential employer.

Changing careers can be stressful, but it can also be a time of exciting personal growth and discovery. We hope that the Field Guides to Finding a New Career not only help you get your bearings in today's employment jungle, but set you on the path to personal fulfillment, happiness, and prosperity.

How to Use This Book

Career Compasses

Each chapter begins with a series of "career compasses" to help you get your bearings and determine if this job is right for you, based on your answers to the self-assessment quiz at the beginning of the book. Does it require a mathematical mindset? Communication skills? Organizational skills? If you're not a "people person," a job requiring you to interact with the public might not be right for you. On the other hand, your organizational skills might be just what are needed in the back office.

Destination

A brief overview, giving you an introduction to the career, briefly explaining what it is, its advantages, why it is so satisfying, its growth potential, and its income potential.

You Are Here

A self-assessment asking you to locate yourself on your journey. Are you working in a related field? Are you working in a field where some skills will transfer? Or are you doing something completely different? In each case, we suggest ways to reapply your skills, gain new ones, and launch yourself on your new career path.

Navigating the Terrain

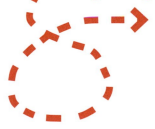

To help you on your way, we have provided a handy map showing the stages in your journey to a new career. "Navigating the Terrain" will show you the road you need to follow to get where you are going. Since the answers are not the same for everyone and every career, we are sure to show how there are multiple ways to get to the same destination.

Organizing Your Expedition

Fleshing out "Navigating the Terrain," we give explicit directions on how to enter this new career: Decide on a destination, scout the terrain, and decide on a path that is right for you. Of course, the answers are not the same for everyone.

Landmarks

People have different needs at different ages. "Landmarks" presents advice specific to the concerns of each age demographic: early career (twenties), mid-career (thirties to forties), senior employees (fifties) and second-career starters (sixties). We address not only issues such as overcoming age discrimination, but also possible concerns of spouses and families (for instance, paying college tuition with reduced income) and keeping up with new technologies.

Essential Gear

Indispensable tips for career-changers on things such as gearing your résumé to a job in a new field, finding contacts and networking, obtaining further education and training, and how to gain experience in the new field.

Notes from the Field

Sometimes it is useful to consult with those who have gone before for insights and advice. "Notes from the Field" presents interviews with career-changers, presenting motivations and methods that you can identify with.

Further Resources

Finally, we give a list of "expedition outfitters" to provide you with further resources and trade resources.

Make the Most of Your Journey

We have spent a decade watching television reports and reading newspaper stories about greed, corruption, and scandals in financial institutions, pharmaceutical companies, and insurance companies. It begs the question: Why would you want to read this book? Why would you want to work alongside a bunch of selfish, greedy people?

Well, you may want to read this book just to see those myths shattered. There is greed and corruption in business and finance. But there is also honor, integrity, and some very smart people who are trying to use their knowledge and expertise to make life better for everyone. In fact the scandals of 2008-09 have opened doors for financially minded people of conscience. Can you have it all? Can you work in a high-paying field and still feel good about yourself? Can you make a difference in the world? In this book you will meet people who can answer "yes" to these questions—people who have switched careers and are now very successful in business and finance, and who are proud of the difference they are making. For example, take vice president of Apple Bank Cynthia Wang, who in Chapter 10 discusses how Apple employees lost business to predatory banks awarding loans to people who did not meet Apple's criteria. "We wondered how they could do it," says Cynthia. "How could they (other banks) offer loans and terms that didn't seem prudent to us?" When we went to press, most of those banks had closed their doors or were begging for government bailouts, and Cynthia and her colleagues were busier than ever. Or listen to John Kaiser, vice president of ACADIA Pharmaceuticals, who in Chapter 6 says, "Pharmaceutical marketing is all about helping doctors help people by getting the *right* drug to the *right* patient." Such sentiments run contrary to the idea that pharmaceutical marketers will sell anything to anybody. "Marketing is communication and education," explains John. As he transitioned from a career in pharmacy to one in marketing, he used his scientific knowledge to make sure physicians were educated about the drugs he marketed.

If you have ever been given bad advice by a financial advisor, meet a few of the people in Chapter 2. Chuck Bender, CPA, MBA, jumped off the fast track at one of the top four accounting firms to try to make a difference in people's lives. Lauren Lindsay has spent years helping victims of Katrina rebuild their finances and their lives. Philip Watson runs his financial planning business the way his dad ran a Western Auto franchise. "People know they can trust me," he states. "My dad would never sell you a car you did not need and I will never try to sell you a financial service you do not need." In fact, Phil is one of a new breed of financial planners who do not sell anything except their time.

For those who want to go further than doing their own jobs with honesty and integrity, this volume covers "watchdog" careers as well. Auditors make sure companies have systems in place to comply with government rules and regulations, and they investigate to weed out fraud or malfeasance. Although many auditors are accountants, not all audits are financial and this growing field is open to people from a variety of backgrounds. Information technology (IT) auditors usually have a background in information systems or computer science. Other professions may also be good jumping off points for this field. Industrial engineers, psychologists, and people experienced in crisis public relations often bring valuable perspectives to this work. The professional associations for auditors—The Institute of Internal Auditors (IIA) and ISACA, formerly known as the Information Systems Audit and Control Association—can help prospective auditors determine what additional education or training will be helpful to them.

Accounting can be a "watchdog" profession too. Forensic accountants work with police and the FBI to investigate crimes such as securities fraud and embezzlement. There are many other opportunities for accountants, however. Management accountants employed by a corporation work side by side with the chief executive officer and other executives to set corporate strategy, foster business growth, increase profitability, and make sure the company complies with tax laws and business regulations. It is no wonder that management accounting is often on the path to corporate leadership. Public accountants come from outside the corporation to audit financial records and may also provide consulting services. Of course many accountants do not want to be part of the corporate culture and instead chose to service small businesses and individuals. If you are interested in accounting but do not want to or cannot currently pursue a bachelor's degree, you may want to consider bookkeeping. Although bookkeeping can be a stepping stone to an accounting career, it is a great destination itself. Bookkeeping offers flexible work options—full or part time for a company, freelancing, or starting your own business.

Those more interested in research and analysis may want to consider a career as a financial analyst or a loan officer. Financial analysts carefully and methodically scrutinize a company's financial statements as part of their evaluation of that company's financial strength and stability. The financial analyst's report on a company usually includes recommendations about whether to buy, sell, or hold that company's stock. But as Catherine Hopkins, CFA, research analyst for Clay Finlay says, "Companies exist for a bigger purpose than their stock." This work requires the ability to look beyond financial data, models, and formulas to evaluate how a company stands in the real world. Is there strong leadership? What about the competition? How will new business regulations and tax laws impact this company? Solid analytical and research skills, an eye for investigation, and good judgment are keys to success. These same skills are also important for loan officers. Loan officers assess a potential borrower's ability to repay a loan. In the case of mortgages, they also evaluate the property under consideration. Loan officers in larger banks may focus on large commercial loans and mortgages, while those who work for small banks or branches usually deal with personal loans and mortgages.

People over 40 may have an edge for two of the professions covered in this book—personal financial advisor and stockbroker. Older advisors and brokers are more likely to benefit from friends with financial resources. An exception to this is the discount broker who usually works in a large call center and is not involved in generating business. Nowadays, in addition to offering investment advice, most financial advisors work as holistic financial planners, addressing all aspects of a client's financial life from college and retirement saving to estate planning and insurance. The scandals of 2008-9 increased peoples' concerns about their money and their wariness of financial advisors. Trusted advisors who really listen to and try to do the best for clients should see many career opportunities.

The insurance industry offers opportunities and usually in-house education for career switchers. Those with an analytical bent may want to consider becoming an insurance underwriter who designs policies based on analysis of individual or group risks. The work of a claims adjuster is quite different. This career involves investigating claims, negotiating settlements for valid claims, and highlighting fraud when it is suspected. People who have experience in the insurance claims being investigated—health professionals for medical insurance claims, auto mechanics for car insurance claims, and those working in construction for property damage claims, for example—have a good head start for this career opportunity. Those with a background in law enforcement have an edge in claims fraud investigation. But many successful claims adjusters work their way up from clerical positions in an insurance company.

The careers in this book offer opportunities for those with different personality types and different levels of education. An MBA or a master's degree in a finance- related field is helpful for some of the professions discussed in this book. But you can start at a lower level and go to school in the evening. Nowadays most MBA programs prefer candidates who have worked in business for a couple of years anyway. In many cases studying for and obtaining certification while you work in the field may be more helpful than a master's degree. This is the case for financial analysts, accountants, auditors, and personal financial advisors. You can also look at the many professions where an MBA is not necessary. Although most professions require a bachelor's degree, you can attend classes in the evening while you work and get on-the-job training during the day. Many large financial institutions offer free in-house education along with on-the-job training. Lauren Lindsay, financial planner, and Vivian Kaufman, stockbroker and advisor, obtained their licenses and certifications by taking advantage of free classes offered by their employers. There are solid professions, such as bookkeeper and claims adjuster, that do not usually require a degree.

Some of the careers described are especially amenable to those wishing to start their own business. Pay special attention to the financial advisors in Chapter 2 and to Jo Duer, bookkeeper, in Chapter 8. Jo taught herself QuickBook and started her own bookkeeping business. Jo feels her ability to engender trust plays a big role in her success. Clients know she has the maturity and integrity to maintain confidentiality. Many accountants and auditors also choose self-employment or start small businesses with other colleagues.

No matter what your image of the business and finance world—men and women in dark suits and briefcases rushing to work at the megacorporation in New York City, or small, casual firms with more interpersonal contact—you will find a wealth of proven information in this book. Read about all the professions and see what sparks your interest. If something makes you think, "Hey, I can do that," or "I would really like to try that," follow the guidance provided. Soon you may find yourself at the forefront of a new career.

Self-Assessment Quiz

I: Relevant Knowledge

1. How many years of specialized training have you had?
   (a) None, it is not required
   (b) Several weeks to several months of training
   (c) A year-long course or other preparation
   (d) Years of preparation in graduate or professional school, or equivalent job experience

2. Would you consider training to obtain certification or other required credentials?
   (a) No
   (b) Yes, but only if it is legally mandated
   (c) Yes, but only if it is the industry standard
   (d) Yes, if it is helpful (even if not mandatory)

3. In terms of achieving success, how would you rate the following qualities in order from least to most important?
   (a) ability, effort, preparation
   (b) ability, preparation, effort
   (c) preparation, ability, effort
   (d) preparation, effort, ability

4. How would you feel about keeping track of current developments in your field?
   (a) I prefer a field where very little changes
   (b) If there were a trade publication, I would like to keep current with that
   (c) I would be willing to regularly recertify my credentials or learn new systems
   (d) I would be willing to aggressively keep myself up-to-date in a field that changes constantly

5. For whatever reason, you have to train a bright young successor to do your job. How quickly will he or she pick it up?
   (a) Very quickly
   (b) He or she can pick up the necessary skills on the job
   (c) With the necessary training he or she should succeed with hard work and concentration
   (d) There is going to be a long breaking-in period—there is no substitute for experience

II: Caring

1. How would you react to the following statement: "Other people are the most important thing in the world?"
   (a) No! Me first!
   (b) I do not really like other people, but I do make time for them
   (c) Yes, but you have to look out for yourself first
   (d) Yes, to such a degree that I often neglect my own well-being

2. Who of the following is the best role model?
   (a) Ayn Rand
   (b) Napoléon Bonaparte
   (c) Bill Gates
   (d) Florence Nightingale

3. How do you feel about pets?
   (a) I do not like animals at all
   (b) Dogs and cats and such are OK, but not for me
   (c) I have a pet, or I wish I did
   (d) I have several pets, and caring for them occupies significant amounts of my time

4. Which of the following sets of professions seems most appealing to you?
   (a) business leader, lawyer, entrepreneur
   (b) politician, police officer, athletic coach
   (c) teacher, religious leader, counselor
   (d) nurse, firefighter, paramedic

5. How well would you have to know someone to give them $100 in a harsh but not life-threatening circumstance? It would have to be...
    (a)   ...a close family member or friend (brother or sister, best friend)
    (b)   ...a more distant friend or relation (second cousin, coworkers)
    (c)   ...an acquaintance (a coworker, someone from a community organization or church)
    (d)   ...a complete stranger

III: Organizational Skills

1. Do you create sub-folders to further categorize the items in your "Pictures" and "Documents" folders on your computer?
    (a)   No
    (b)   Yes, but I do not use them consistently
    (c)   Yes, and I use them consistently
    (d)   Yes, and I also do so with my e-mail and music library

2. How do you keep track of your personal finances?
    (a)   I do not, and I am never quite sure how much money is in my checking account
    (b)   I do not really, but I always check my online banking to make sure I have money
    (c)   I am generally very good about budgeting and keeping track of my expenses, but sometimes I make mistakes
    (d)   I do things such as meticulously balance my checkbook, fill out Excel spreadsheets of my monthly expenses, and file my receipts

3. Do you systematically order commonly used items in your kitchen?
    (a)   My kitchen is a mess
    (b)   I can generally find things when I need them
    (c)   A place for everything, and everything in its place
    (d)   Yes, I rigorously order my kitchen and do things like alphabetize spices and herbal teas

4. How do you do your laundry?
    (a)   I cram it in any old way
    (b)   I separate whites and colors

(c)   I separate whites and colors, plus whether it gets dried

(d)   Not only do I separate whites and colors and drying or non-drying, I organize things by type of clothes or some other system

5.   Can you work in clutter?
(a)   Yes, in fact I feel energized by the mess
(b)   A little clutter never hurt anyone
(c)   No, it drives me insane
(d)   Not only does my workspace need to be neat, so does that of everyone around me

IV: Communication Skills

1.   Do people ask you to speak up, not mumble, or repeat yourself?
(a)   All the time
(b)   Often
(c)   Sometimes
(d)   Never

2.   How do you feel about speaking in public?
(a)   It terrifies me
(b)   I can give a speech or presentation if I have to, but it is awkward
(c)   No problem!
(d)   I frequently give lectures and addresses, and I am very good at it

3.   What's the difference between *their, they're,* and *there*?
(a)   I do not know
(b)   I know there is a difference, but I make mistakes in usage
(c)   I know the difference, but I cannot articulate it
(d)   *Their* is the third-person possessive, *they're* is a contraction for *they are,* and *there* is a deictic adverb meaning "in that place"

4.   Do you avoid writing long letters or e-mails because you are ashamed of your spelling, punctuation, and grammatical mistakes?
(a)   Yes
(b)   Yes, but I am either trying to improve or just do not care what people think

    (c)   The few mistakes I make are easily overlooked

    (d)   Save for the occasional typo, I do not ever make mistakes in usage

5.   Which choice best characterizes the most challenging book you are willing to read in your spare time?

    (a)   I do not read

    (b)   Light fiction reading such as the Harry Potter series, *The Da Vinci Code*, or mass-market paperbacks

    (c)   Literary fiction or mass-market nonfiction such as history or biography

    (d)   Long treatises on technical, academic, or scientific subjects

V: Mathematical Skills

1.   Do spreadsheets make you nervous?

    (a)   Yes, and I do not use them at all

    (b)   I can perform some simple tasks, but I feel that I should leave them to people who are better-qualified than myself

    (c)   I feel that I am a better-than-average spreadsheet user

    (d)   My job requires that I be very proficient with them

2.   What is the highest level math class you have ever taken?

    (a)   I flunked high-school algebra

    (b)   Trigonometry or pre-calculus

    (c)   College calculus or statistics

    (d)   Advanced college mathematics

3.   Would you rather make a presentation in words or using numbers and figures?

    (a)   Definitely in words

    (b)   In words, but I could throw in some simple figures and statistics if I had to

    (c)   I could strike a balance between the two

    (d)   Using numbers as much as possible; they are much more precise

4.   Cover the answers below with a sheet of paper, and then solve the following word problem: Mary has been legally able to vote for exactly half her life. Her husband John is three years older than she. Next year,

their son Harvey will be exactly one-quarter of John's age. How old was Mary when Harvey was born?
(a) I couldn't work out the answer
(b) 25
(c) 26
(d) 27

5. Cover the answers below with a sheet of paper, and then solve the following word problem: There are seven children on a school bus. Each child has seven book bags. Each bag has seven big cats in it. Each cat has seven kittens. How many legs are there on the bus?
(a) I couldn't work out the answer
(b) 2,415
(c) 16,821
(d) 10,990

VI: Ability to Manage Stress

1. It is the end of the working day, you have 20 minutes to finish an hour-long job, and you are scheduled to pick up your children. Your supervisor asks you why you are not finished. You:
(a) Have a panic attack
(b) Frantically redouble your efforts
(c) Calmly tell her you need more time, make arrangements to have someone else pick up the kids, and work on the project past closing time
(d) Calmly tell her that you need more time to do it right and that you have to leave, or ask if you can release this flawed version tonight

2. When you are stressed, do you tend to:
(a) Feel helpless, develop tightness in your chest, break out in cold sweats, or have other extreme, debilitating physiological symptoms?
(b) Get irritable and develop a hair-trigger temper, drink too much, obsess over the problem, or exhibit other "normal" signs of stress?
(c) Try to relax, keep your cool, and act as if there is no problem
(d) Take deep, cleansing breaths and actively try to overcome the feelings of stress

3. The last time I was so angry or frazzled that I lost my composure was:
    (a) Last week or more recently
    (b) Last month
    (c) Over a year ago
    (d) So long ago I cannot remember

4. Which of the following describes you?
    (a) Stress is a major disruption in my life, people have spoken to me about my anger management issues, or I am on medication for my anxiety and stress
    (b) I get anxious and stressed out easily
    (c) Sometimes life can be a challenge, but you have to climb that mountain!
    (d) I am generally easygoing

5. What is your ideal vacation?
    (a) I do not take vacations; I feel my work life is too demanding
    (b) I would just like to be alone, with no one bothering me
    (c) I would like to do something not too demanding, like a cruise, with friends and family
    (d) I am an adventurer; I want to do exciting (or even dangerous) things and visit foreign lands

Scoring:

For each category...

For every answer of *a*, add zero points to your score.
For every answer of *b*, add ten points to your score.
For every answer of *c*, add fifteen points to your score.
For every answer of *d*, add twenty points to your score.

The result is your percentage in that category.

Financial Analyst

Career Compasses

Guide yourself to a career as a financial analyst.

Mathematical Skills to understand complex financial data, financial models, and statistics (50%)

Relevant Knowledge of trends in business, economics, and government that may impact corporate performance (20%)

Communication Skills to explain complex financial concepts and present written and verbal reports (20%)

Ability to Manage Stress under deadline pressure (10%)

Destination: Financial Analyst

The newspaper headlines scream, "XYZ Fortune 100 Company reports third quarter earnings better than expected." The news story goes on to say that financial analysts predict continued growth from this company over the next quarter. How can they make that prediction? Financial analysts—also known as securities analysts or investment analysts—research, analyze, and report on companies' economic strength and potential. They carefully scrutinize financial statements, question chief executive officers and chief financial officers, and consider how external factors-business regulations and competition, new tax laws, and the overall economy and sociopolitical trends-may influence a company's success. Analysts usually track the same companies and/or sectors (groups of similar companies, such as technology or pharmaceuticals) over time so they have a solid understanding of how each company stands in relation to others in the same field. Financial analysts prepare detailed reports of their findings with well-researched interpretations of the information. Their reports usually include recommendations about whether to buy, sell, or hold stock in these companies. In addition to written reports, financial analysts often present their findings verbally in executive meetings. Their analyses of a company's financial viability help determine whether their employers invest in that company.

Financial analysts work wherever people make decisions about investing. At large investment banks and other investment firms, mutual funds, pension funds, and charities with endowments, the focus is generally on whether to buy, sell, or hold equities and bonds. Some financial analysts work for insurance companies or commercial or savings banks without investment divisions. In these businesses, analysts evaluate a company's risk of defaulting on a loan or filing claims on an insurance policy. Other financial analysts, sometimes called ratings analysts, rate a company or government's ability to repay its debt. International banks also employ financial analysts called country analysts. These analysts evaluate a

Essential Gear

Chartered Financial Analyst (CFA) certification. To study for CFA certification from CFA Institute, you must have a bachelor's degree or equivalent. More than half CFA Institute members have a master's degree, law degree, or post-graduate diploma. This is a self-study program. You must sequentially study three intensive course syllabi, which focus on the investment decision-making process and are similar to what you would study in a master's level program, and take three rigorous examinations (Levels I, II, III). These exams are given annually (Level I is given twice a year) at various locations throughout the United States and around the world. You can find a list at the CFA Web site. The CFA Institute provides members with ongoing professional development through publications, Web casts, and conferences. Also consider a course, such as Kaplan Schweser (http://www.schweser.com) or Stalla (http://www.stalla.com), to help you prepare for the exam.

country's economic stability the way the other analysts evaluate a corporation's economic strength. Some analysts work for fund managers or portfolio managers. These analysts assess the overall risk of a given portfolio and make recommendations or decisions about diversification. Many large corporations evaluated by financial analysts employ their own financial analysts to prepare external reports or assist in mergers and acquisitions.

If this type of work sounds interesting to you, and you wish to enter a rapidly growing field with good pay and many opportunities for advancement, then the time is right to consider a career as a financial analyst. Although there are employment opportunities worldwide, investment-related jobs tend to be concentrated in major financial centers, such as New York, Chicago, Los Angeles, London, and Hong Kong. Despite the growing need for financial analysts, however, there is stiff competition for jobs. As you might imagine, firms want to make sure they have the best people providing such important information. The financial analyst's reports influence major (often multibillion-dollar) financial decisions, such as the buying or selling of equities, underwriting of loans or insurance policies, or rating of government and corporate bonds.

Essential Gear

Chartered Market Analyst (CMA) designation. The CMA designation from the International Academy of Financial Managers (IAFM) requires a combination of an academic degree (bachelor's or master's in finance, tax, accounting, financial services, insurance, or law; or a CPA, MBA, MS, Ph.D., or JD), relevant work experience, and completion of an IAFM-sanctioned Executive Training Course. Courses are available online and at various locations throughout the country and around the world. You will need less work experience and course work if you have a master's in finance or business than if you have a BBA. The IAFM requires 15 hours of continuing education annually in order to maintain certification.

Consequently, strong credentials are essential. Many financial analysts have an MBA or a master's degree in a financial field, such as finance or accounting. If you have a bachelor's degree you can obtain appropriate credentials by pursuing a master's degree, ideally from an accredited business school, or by obtaining certification through one of the professional associations, CFA (Chartered Financial Analyst) Institute or The International Academy of Financial Managers (IAFM). The financial analyst's education does not end with a degree or certification. You must keep up with constantly changing factors that influence the financial strength of companies and/or governments, such as general economic conditions, tax laws, other federal regulations, and geopolitical conditions.

There are two other ways to break into this field. You might apply for an apprentice position at one of the major investment banks. These programs are extremely competitive. If you are accepted, however, the firm puts you through an intense two-year training program. Alternatively, if you have a degree and relevant work experience in a particular sector, such as technology or pharmaceuticals, an investment firm might be willing to provide on-the-job financial training. Your expertise in that sector combined with financial training would give you added insight in to the workings of those companies.

What is it like once you become a financial analyst? You should be prepared to work fairly long hours, particularly at times of the year when corporations release earnings reports. At those times there is also considerable deadline pressure. The importance of providing accurate analysis also makes this a stressful job for many people. The style of work varies at different investment institutions and from analyst to analyst. Some analysts focus primarily on financial data. Others focus more on the company itself, its product(s), and how it stands in the field. Both aspects are integrated into any meaningful decisions. If you work for a large investment firm, you are likely to have a more thorough involvement with a smaller number of equities and your team will develop relationships with the chief executive officers (CEOs) and chief financial officers (CFOs) of these companies. In a smaller investment house you may cover a much larger number of companies and include the reports from the more specialized analysts in your assessments. In a smaller house you will talk to some company managers, but also glean information from a variety of sources including other analysts, company meetings, general news, consumer groups, and economic data.

Regardless of the size of the firm, financial analysts use spreadsheets, mathematical formulas, and statistical software packages to help them analyze data and identify trends. Despite this, they must always remember to look up from the computer and take a broader view of the company they are evaluating. They need to understand the company's management style, its products, and its relationship to its competitors, as well as see the company in the context of the global economy. This combination of attention to mathematical detail with a broad world-view is what makes the job so challenging and constantly changing.

You Are Here

How will you fare as a financial analyst?

Do people refer to you as a "numbers person?" Strong mathematical skills and knowledge of complex mathematical concepts and strategies are the cornerstones of financial analysis. Financial analysts use algebra, statistics, and sometimes calculus to model and predict a company's economic strength.

Navigating the Terrain

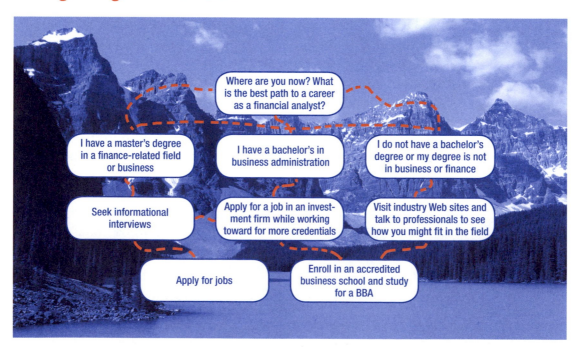

Where are you now? What is the best path to a career as a financial analyst?

I have a master's degree in a finance-related field or business

I have a bachelor's in business administration

I do not have a bachelor's degree or my degree is not in business or finance

Seek informational interviews

Apply for a job in an investment firm while working toward for more credentials

Visit industry Web sites and talk to professionals to see how you might fit in the field

Apply for jobs

Enroll in an accredited business school and study for a BBA

Do you like to do research? You will not only need to carefully scrutinize whatever financial statements the company gives you, but search for other sources to help you develop an evaluation of that company. Other sources might be business and world news, professional conferences, data from other analysts, and interviews with corporate executives. You will need to pull together all of this information in order to make your recommendations, sifting through many different leads in search of the company's true financial picture.

Do you combine self-confidence with a dose of humility? You must have the confidence to present your recommendations to groups of executives who will use this information to make major financial decisions. But overconfidence can lead to mistakes. The markets frequently surprise the most seasoned experts, and you need to carefully think about what you see and not assume things that you do not know.

Organizing Your Expedition

You will find many different routes can take you to a career as a financial analyst.

Decide on a destination. Think about the work environment you would like. Most jobs will be in investment banks or independent investment firms. Many of the larger investment institutions offer apprentice courses, and you have the opportunity to learn firsthand from expert analysts. Competition to get in is keen, however, and the work often involves long hours and a lot of stress. The environment is usually a bit less stressful in a smaller, boutique-type investment house. If you like the nonprofit arena, you might consider helping a charity grow its endowment by investing in strong equities. Some analysts work for the corporations being evaluated by other analysts. These jobs are often more low-key but can become quite pressured if there is a merger or acquisition. Insurance companies and savings banks are alternative work places.

Scout the terrain. Get an inside view of different work settings. Talk to financial analysts from different types of companies to get a sense of what their jobs entail. One way to meet financial analysts is to go to so-

Notes from the Field

Catherine C. Hopkins, CFA
Research analyst, Clay Finlay LLC
New York, New York

What were you doing before you became a financial analyst?

I attended the Robins School of Business at the University of Richmond and graduated with a BSBA in marketing and international business. After graduation, I moved to New York City and worked for The David Green Organization, a site selection firm for corporate meeting planners. I worked directly under the vice president of sales as an intermediary between the in-house meeting planners for large corporations and the hotels, locating event space and negotiating the contract terms between our clients and the hotels. During my time at David Green, I learned a great deal about the business world and my likes and dislikes. Negotiating contracts and understanding the client's needs in order to find the right property was very rewarding. However, the sales aspect of the work was not as exciting.

I became interested in my current field after being contacted by a recruiter about an opportunity at Clay Finlay, a focused global equity boutique, that manages global, international, and regional equity mandates on behalf of public and corporate institutions, endowments, and foundations. My first position at Clay Finlay was on the operations and compliance side of the business. While a four-year undergraduate degree was required, it was not necessary for it to be in finance.

Why did you decide to become a financial analyst?

I knew I liked analytical work, and my boss/mentor at Clay Finlay suggested that I might like research. After speaking with the portfolio managers and other analysts at Clay Finlay, the work sounded interesting to me.

cial networking functions and job fairs. To find out about both, go to the CFA Institute Web site and click on "Societies." Contact the society nearest you to find out about these functions in your area. Another way to get the inside scoop is to get a job in any department of an investment firm. You will gain work experience (essential for certification), make contacts,

What was involved in terms of education/training and getting your first job?

While working in the operations area, I began to study for Level I of the Chartered Financial Analyst (CFA) exam. The preparation continued to provide me with significant insight into a financial analyst's work. The course work also allowed me to obtain the training I needed without going back to school and sacrificing income.

A bachelor's degree (or equivalent) is necessary to sit for the first level of the CFA exam. CFA Institute provides a syllabus and curriculum along with a guide of how many hours a week to study. In addition, I took courses through both Stalla® and Kaplan Schweser, which I found kept me on pace. The prep courses offered by both Stalla and Schweser are independent of CFA Institute. I began studying for Level I in January and completed the exam in June of that year. Although the Level I exam is administered in both June and December, Level II and III exams are only offered in June. While continuing with the CFA program I moved to the research side as a junior analyst, subsequently received my charter and continue to work as a research analyst.

What are the keys to success as a financial analyst?

Hard work tops the list. An enormous amount of self-study, focus, and discipline goes into obtaining the CFA designation. This prepares you for the diligence needed to be a good financial analyst. It is important to pay close attention to details as you evaluate a company's financial statements and develop financial models. However, a good analyst must also understand the overall picture of the organization and its industry. Why is a company successful or unsuccessful? Companies exist for a bigger purpose than their stock and it is important not to lose sight of that, especially as a fundamental analyst. Finally, humility is absolutely essential. The minute your ego plays a role, the market will prove you wrong. Humility keeps you grounded and hopefully prevents you from making fundamental mistakes by being overconfident.

and learn more about what analysts do. You will also find out what that firm prefers in terms of financial analyst credentials. Do they insist on a master's degree or is a bachelor's degree sufficient? Which certification do they prefer? There may be opportunities for transfer once you obtain the appropriate credentials.

Find the path that's right for you. When thinking about the work setting you prefer, you will need to consider whether or not you are open to relocating. Positions in major investment firms are located in major financial hubs, such as New York, San Francisco, Hong Kong, and London. But a city near you may have opportunities as well. Is there a major corporation headquartered in your area that would need an inside financial analyst? What about your local savings bank? Remember, financial analysts also evaluate an individual or company's ability to repay a loan. As you consider the possibility of relocating, find out where jobs are located by checking job listings on the Web. If you have considerable experience in a sector of the market (the pharmaceutical industry, for example) some investment firms may covet your "inside knowledge" of that sector and be willing to train you as an analyst.

Go back to school. Keep in mind that school does not have to be full time. In addition to earning a living, you will glean necessary experience if you get a job in an investment firm while you pursue your education. Certification and many master's programs require several years of relevant work experience. If you already have an MBA or a master's in a finance-related field, you can begin to apply for jobs as a financial analyst.

If you think you need additional knowledge of financial strategies and investment decision-making, you can look for study opportunities through the International Academy of Financial Management or CFA Institute. Many analysts with masters' degrees go on to obtain certification as well.

Landmarks

If you are in your twenties . . . Look for a job at an investment firm so you can gain experience and talk to financial analysts there about their jobs. At this point, if you do not already have a master's in a finance-related field or business, you should go for it or for CFA or CMA certification.

If you are in your thirties or forties . . . If your financial needs are modest and you are able to start at the bottom again, you should look for any job available at an investment firm while you pursue the education or certification you need. If you have a family and need income from your current better-paying job, you might want to start to network. Go to job fairs and social networking functions. Meanwhile, pursue whatever educational or certification requirements are necessary for you—bachelor's degree, master's degree, or certification. As you gain the necessary credentials, you can begin a job search for a financial analyst position. This is also a good time to become a financial analyst if you have been accruing credentials in a field of value to an investment firm, such as pharmaceuticals or technology.

If you are in your fifties . . . The major investment houses tend to look toward younger people who often demand lower salaries. However, this field is not closed to you if you pursue the educational and/or certification requirements. If you have a good position in a sector of interest to investors, you can capitalize on that experience. If you are a good mathematician, perhaps a former math teacher or accountant, you may be able to transfer your skills and find a job at an insurance company, savings bank, or local business.

If you are over sixty . . . You may want to look for a job on the financial analyst's team. In larger institutions, research assistants and associate analysts often help with input gathering. If you do have related experience in math or accounting, local banks and businesses may provide a way for you to transfer your skills.

Further Resources

The **CFA Institute** is a global membership association for investment professionals with 136 member societies. Their Web site includes profiles of members, a list of member societies, and course syllabi for the three levels of the exam necessary for CFA designation. http://www.cfainstitute.org

The **International Academy of Financial Managers (IAFM)** is a broader base organization, offering eight board certifications for different types of financial professionals worldwide. Founded as a global professional organization for highly educated individuals or industry experts, the IAFM requires a degree from an accredited business school for membership. http://www.aafm.org

Personal Financial Advisor

Personal Financial Advisor

Career Compasses

Guide yourself to a career as a personal financial advisor.

Relevant Knowledge to stay current on factors that influence your clients' financial plans and investments, such as changes in tax laws and stock market fluctuations (40%)

Mathematical Skills to help clients develop budget and savings plans and to allocate percentages of clients' portfolios to different investments (10%)

Communication Skills to listen carefully to your clients' needs and clearly explain their choices (40%)

Ability to Manage Stress when the market is down and clients are worried about their investments (10%)

Destination: Personal Financial Advisor

Accountants, teachers, guitar players, dentists, computer technicians, insurance salespersons, stockbrokers, MBAs, ministers, scientists, pig farmers, stay-at-home moms. People from all professions have switched careers to become personal financial advisors. One study by the Financial Planning Association Research Center found that about one-third of advisors interviewed had come from another profession. If this work interests you, there are numerous resources nationwide to help you acquire the education and credentials you need. What you must bring to the picture is a commitment to listen empathically to your client and an ability to absorb a stream of constantly changing data (investment risks, tax laws and regulations, and the like) that impacts the client's financial decisions.

One reason this field attracts people from so many different backgrounds is because there are so many different ways to practice. Some personal financial advisors focus primarily on investment advice. These people are also called investment advisors, money managers, or private bankers. Nowadays, however, the trend is toward advisors who offer comprehensive (sometimes called holistic) financial planning, including spending/saving/debt management advice, portfolio design, investment advice, college savings plans, estate plans, retirement plans, and insurance coverage. These advisors are often called personal financial planners or, depending on the firm and clientele, wealth managers.

> ## Essential Gear
>
> **Continuing education.** Ongoing education about changes in rules and regulations impacting investments, taxes, insurance, retirement plans, and estate planning, is essential for financial advisors. All of the organizations mentioned in this section—FPA, NAPFA, and IMCA—provide programs to help you keep up-to-date. In addition, once you obtain the series 65 license, FINRA will begin to regularly email you notices of educational events.

The work setting for personal financial advisors varies greatly, from a small home office to huge investment firm. Most advisors who provide comprehensive planning work for independent financial advisory firms (sometimes called wealth-management firms), for themselves, or with a partner or two. There are also financial advisors working for banks, broker-dealers, mutual fund companies, pension funds, and insurance companies. Most of these advisors focus on investments and money management, but some now offer comprehensive planning as well.

There is also variation in the way advisors are compensated. Some work for a fee only, some for a fee plus commission on the sale of products such as mutual funds and insurance, and some for commission only. Advisors who work for a fee-only advisory firm sometimes receive salary plus bonus. To minimize conflicts of interest, fee-based compensation (primarily fee plus some commission) is becoming the industry standard, according to a five-year study by Cerulli Associates for the Financial Planning Association. Seeking to completely eliminate conflict of interest, an increasing number of comprehensive planners have adopted a fee-only pay structure. Many advisors, including fee-only planners, also manage the client's investments on an ongoing basis and receive a percentage (generally around 1 percent) of the client's assets under management (AUM). In this model, the advisor's compensation grows or declines as the client's assets grow or decline. Some fee-only planners feel the fee for AUM still presents a potential for conflict of interest. They suggest that an advisor might be tempted to advise a client not to buy a house since that money would no longer be part of the AUM fee. These planners charge a flat retainer instead.

The process of developing a financial plan for a client often proceeds as follows: First, a free consultation with the client lets him or her know how you work and your method of compensation. Second, you have an in-person interview (usually two to four hours) and follow-up phone calls to learn everything you can about your client's finances, life goals, estate and retirement plans, and insurance coverage. You then analyze this information, design the plan, and present it to the client, discussing and modifying as needed. Once you have the client's authorization, you implement and manage the plan by purchasing securities, usually through an independent broker-dealer, and arranging meetings with estate attorneys and insurance agents. Finally, ongoing consultation—meeting with the client regularly to review the plan and adapt it to reflect changes in the client's life—is the essential ingredient for keeping the plan viable and up-to-date.

Essential Gear

Registration and licenses. To give investment advice, you will either need to register with the Securities and Exchange Commission (SEC) as a Registered Investment Advisor (RIA) or work for a firm that is registered. Find more information at http://www.sec.gov/divisions/investment/iard/register.shtml. Many advisors also obtain the series 65 license from the Financial Industry Regulatory Authority (FINRA). To get this license you must pass a 130-question exam on investment products, retirement planning, business ethics, securities rules and regulations, and other topics. For information on study materials, dates, and locations of testing sites go to http:///www.finra.org.

Does this work sound interesting to you? If it does, now is a great time to switch careers to this rapidly growing field. The aging of the baby boomer generation is dramatically increasing the need for financial advisors who can help boomers plan for retirement and manage their money. Increasing complexity and volatility in the financial market is also driving more and more people to seek expert help. The Bureau of Labor Statistics projects that the number of personal financial advisors will grow by 41 percent over the next decade, making this one of the 10 fastest growing occupations in the country. But magazine articles and television commentators have been warning people to carefully scrutinize potential advisors before trusting one with their money. You will therefore need solid credentials to compete in this environment. Advisors must have a bachelor's degree and many have a master's degree. An increasing number study for further certification.

What may not be immediately apparent from the job description is the satisfaction many financial advisors get from their ability to help oth-

Navigating the Terrain

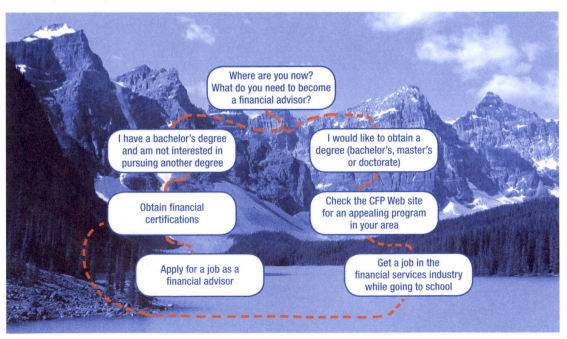

Where are you now? What do you need to become a financial advisor?

I have a bachelor's degree and am not interested in pursuing another degree

I would like to obtain a degree (bachelor's, master's or doctorate)

Obtain financial certifications

Check the CFP Web site for an appealing program in your area

Apply for a job as a financial advisor

Get a job in the financial services industry while going to school

ers. Take Certified Financial Planner (CFP) Steven Young, who looked for a financial advisor to help him invest money from the sale of his pig farm. He was appalled at the advice he got from three planners and decided to study financial planning himself. Now he feels he provides a needed service to others. When his father died, Philip Watson, a guitarist, sought financial advice for his mother. He was so disappointed by the advice he got that he went to study for a certificate in financial planning. Now he gets satisfaction from giving people the type of advice he wishes had been available to him. Chuck Bender, MBA, CPA, had a successful career working for one of the nation's top accounting firms and then for a Fortune 500 corporation. But something was missing. He comments, "If I did not show up for work, if my company's product did not exist, what difference would it make? I was looking for a way to make an impact on people's lives." Chuck now works for a fee-only financial planning firm where the mission statement is "to help relieve our clients of the stress and burden of money management so they can focus on something more important: relationships."

You Are Here

You can start out from almost anywhere and reach this destination.

Do you work in a related financial field? Although not a prerequisite, a degree and experience in accounting, business, investments, insurance, or another area of finance can give you a head start. Try to find a position at an advisory firm that uses your existing skills while you learn the planning part of the business from your colleagues. While working at the Financial Consulate, an advisory firm in Baltimore, Maryland, Chuck Bender, MBA, CPA, learned from his boss and colleagues while studying for his certificate in financial planning. Tom Carstens, a partner at Lenox Advisors in New York City, feels that the best way to become the type of advisor you want to be is to "watch and learn from someone you respect in the profession."

Do you work in an unrelated field? Think about how your skills might benefit you as a financial advisor. Lauren Lindsay, CFP, says her teaching experience helps her educate her clients about their finances. Ste-

Notes from the Field
Lauren G. Lindsay, CFP
Personal Financial Advisors, LLC
Covington, Louisiana

What were you doing before you became a personal financial advisor?

I taught inner city kids in London for five years. Then I came back to the United States and taught for a year in my home state of Massachusetts.

Why did you decide to become a personal financial advisor?

I loved teaching, loved the kids, but I hated the politics. When I came back to the United States the state of Massachusetts would not recognize my master's degree from the University of London. They wanted me to shell out $30,000 and go back for another graduate degree. I started to look for another job (in Boston) and no one would hire me. They all said, "You have teaching experience but nothing else." The only job I got offered was to answer telephones for 401K participants at Putnam in Boston. It was a huge pay cut from teaching, so you can imagine how bad it was. But Putnam offered opportunities to get promoted quickly if you took classes. When I was there six months I started working toward my CFP, and Putnam paid for my classes. While I was at Putnam I also won a sales pitch contest. I beat out people who did sales for a living. To me a sales pitch was like doing a lesson plan, but to a much more willing audience. They actually sit in their seats and do not throw things at you. When the sales pitch was so successful I realized those skills could be transferred to business. That is when it all started

ven Young, CFP, says he ran his pig farm as a business and those same skills helped him launch a successful financial planning business. Philip Watson, CFP, credits the values learned from his small business-owner father for his ability to listen to his clients and understand their needs. "When I was a kid I would listen to my dad question his customers to find out what they really needed. He did not try to sell them what cost the most. His customers trusted him."

to come together for me, when I realized I could be a good personal financial advisor.

What was involved in terms of education/training and getting your first job?

Putnam provided a lot of in-house education, and they paid for me to take evening classes at Merrimack College in Andover, Massachusetts, to prepare for the CFP exam. When I left Putnam I began doing corporate education seminars on 401K plans. People waited in line their entire lunch hour to ask me questions. I started doing financial planning for some of the people I met through these seminars. I would meet people at my house, at Starbucks, at the library. Eventually I rented a small office. My practice grew for five years. When I decided to move to Louisiana with my husband, I sold my firm for a good amount of money. In Louisiana, I joined a one-person firm that had been in existence for 30 years.

What are the keys to success as a personal financial advisor?

Listening skills are most important. Post-Katrina, people who had lost everything were coming to me. I booked a session with a therapist to ask him what to tell these people, how to help them. He said, "You know how to listen, right?" Listening helps me understand what my client needs and wants. Education is of paramount importance too. I like to make sure my clients understand the context of my advice and recommendations.

My own education is vital as well. I do at least one Web seminar a week to keep up with changes that can impact my clients.

Are you a good listener? Good listening skills are essential in order to design a financial plan that is suited to your client's needs. You need to encourage your client to talk freely so that you get to know him/her as a person. By listening closely you will glean information about your client's real attitude toward money, which may be different from what he or she told you at the beginning of your discussion. Every advisor interviewed for this chapter cited listening as the most important skill for success.

Organizing Your Expedition

There are several interesting paths open to people who want to become personal financial advisors.

Decide on a destination. You need to know where you are headed in order to figure out the right path. Ask yourself the following questions: Do I want to work for an established company or do I want to go in to my own business? What type of compensation would be best for me—fee only, fee plus commission, commission only, or salary plus bonus? Do I want to offer investment advice or do I want to provide comprehensive financial planning? Consider the pros and cons of working for an established company versus starting your own business. Although most companies pay advisors commission only, they often offer a base salary for six months and a prospective client list. In addition many large companies provide free educational programs. If you would like to have your own business, consider whether you would prefer to work alone or with a partner. As a solo practitioner you are free to do things exactly as you please, and you can start with no overhead in a small home office. But it will probably take at least three years before you generate a livable income, and you will have to market your services.

Scout the terrain. The great news is that personal financial advisors or planners are needed everywhere there are people who need help planning and managing their money. If you want to work for a broker-dealer or major investment bank, you will have more opportunities in a big city. However, you will find local banks that offer advisory services, insurance companies, and advisory firms almost anywhere. When looking for a job or planning your own business, you may want to consider the type of client you would like to service. Some financial advisors, also known as wealth managers or private bankers, work with relatively affluent clients and focus on maximizing and maintaining wealth. Other advisors prefer working with middle-income clients. They help widows and widowers who have never "handled money before" learn how to manage their finances, or assist people in figuring out how to finance their retirements or maximize the money they can leave for their children and grandchildren.

Find the path that's right for you. If you have a bachelor's degree and you want to work for an established firm, you can begin to job hunt before you obtain certification or licenses. Try to find an employer who will provide educational opportunities to help you prepare for a series 65 license, the investment advisor license offered by the Financial Industry Regulatory Authority (FINRA), or CFP certification. Contact FINRA to find out about preparatory courses for the licensing exam. Also contact the CFP Board of Standards to learn about courses to study for certification. If you decide to start your own business, you will need to register with the Securities and Exchange Commission (SEC), or with your state agency if you will be handling under $25 million in assets. Either way, you can obtain the necessary forms from the SEC Web site.

Essential Gear

Certified Financial Planner (CFP) certification. Studying for this certification is a great way to acquire the knowledge you need to practice as a financial advisor, and the CFP credential will help demonstrate your competence to clients. To be certified, you must have a bachelor's degree, complete a course of study, pass a rigorous exam, and have three years of relevant experience. You will find information on educational programs to prepare you for certification alone or in conjunction with a bachelor's, master's, or doctoral degree on the CFP Web site at http://www.cfp.net/become/examdetails.asp.

Go back to school. If you do not have a bachelor's degree, would like to study financial planning in conjunction with a bachelor's, master's, or doctoral degree program, or if you simply prefer learning in a classroom setting, there are numerous university-based financial planning programs across the country. You will find these listed on the Financial Planning Association Web site. If you are doing fee-only planning, you may want to pursue the National Association of Personal Financial Advisors (NAPFA) designation. If you plan to focus on wealth management you may want to eventually study for additional certifications from the Investment Management Consultants Association (IMCA). IMCA offers the Certified Investment Management Analyst (CIMA) designation and the Chartered Private Wealth Advisor (CPWA) designation. These designations require prolonged study, including onsite classes at leading business schools and exams. Currently, only 2 percent of advisors have the CIMA certification, according to Cerulli Associates.

Landmarks

If you are in your twenties . . . Try to get a job, any job, for a company in the financial arena that offers educational opportunities. Many large mutual fund and brokerage companies have extensive educational offerings for employees. Some of these firms provide the courses you need to prepare for licensing exams.

If you are in your thirties or forties . . . If your current income is necessary, start to study financial planning while working at your current job. Look at the CFP Web site and pick a course of study that seems right for you, that fits with your schedule and other educational goals. You may then want to get a job at an advisory firm, bank, or broker-dealer. At this age, you have the maturity to consider starting your own business alone or with a partner once you have taken the appropriate courses in financial planning.

If you are in your fifties . . . You are the age of most financial planners today, according to data from the Financial Planning Association Research Center. The advice for those in their thirties and forties applies to you as well. You also have significant life experience, which makes it easier to gain the trust of your clients.

If you are over sixty . . . You should do very well with clients nearing or in retirement who feel you can understand their financial needs. Follow the advice for those in their fifties, but try to build your business by giving lectures on retirement planning to community organizations.

Further Resources

The **Financial Planning Association (FPA)** is a professional membership organization for financial advisors. The Web site is a great place to find out more about becoming a financial advisor, look for ongoing educational offerings, jobs, and mentors.   http:// www.fpanet.org

The **Certified Financial Planner Board of Standards** reviews educational offerings to determine if they meet the standards to prepare advisors for certification. You can search this Web site to find board-registered educational offerings in your area and to find out more about the CFP Certification Examination.   http://www.cfp.net

Investment Management Consultants Association (IMCA), a professional organization for financial advisors who specialize in investment consulting and wealth management, provides monthly educational offerings and administers the courses and exams necessary for the CIMA and CPWA credentials.   http://www.imca.org

The **Securities and Exchange Commission (SEC)** registers advisory companies. Their Web site has information about federal and state registration.   http://www.sec.gov

The **Financial Services Regulatory Authority (FINRA)** offers training courses, administers licensing exams, and provides ongoing professional education opportunities.   http://www.finra.org

The **National Association of Personal Financial Advisors (NAPFA)** is the professional membership organization for comprehensive fee-only planners. The Web site features a job search and planner search.   http://www.napfa.org

Accountant

Accountant

Career Compasses

What will it take to become an accountant?

Relevant Knowledge of accounting practices, tax law, and business rules and regulations (25%)

Mathematical Skills to prepare and analyze financial reports (40%)

Communication Skills to convey your recommendations to clients, bosses, or coworkers 20%

Ability to Manage Stress with multiple deadlines a year and often handling several projects at the same time (10%)

Destination: Accountant

The days when people put "accounting" and "dull" in the same sentence are over. Now the career, which attracts people because of its stability and in spite of its tedium, has evolved in to one of the more exciting and challenging career paths available. It is also a career path with an increasing number of stimulating job opportunities. The Bureau of Labor Statistics projects that the job market for accountants will grow significantly over the next decade. Growth will be driven by an increase in the number of businesses and a need for these businesses to comply with constantly changing financial rules and regulations.

There are different branches of accounting. Management accountants—also called cost, managerial, industrial, corporate, or private accountants—work as part of the executive team of a corporation, advising the chief executive officer on the financial implications of all business decisions. They help the chief executive officer strategize, grow the business, increase profitability, and comply with tax laws and other business regulations. Management accountants design cost-effective business processes and set up internal controls to protect the company from fraud, embezzlement, or other wrongdoing. As an experienced management accountant you might handle or oversee all the accounting functions for a small to medium size business, or you might work in a specific area of accounting (financial analysis, planning and budgeting, cost accounting, internal auditing) for a large corporation. When you see the integral role the management accountant plays in making a business successful, you can understand why this is often a path to the very top. Management accountants may become chief financial officers and even chief executive officers.

Essential Gear

Certified Government Financial Manager (CGFM) designation. The Advancing Government Accountability (AGA), the professional association for government accountants, offers the CGFM designation to eligible applicants. Certification requires you to pass an exam, have a bachelor's degree from an accredited university (including at least 24 credit hours in accounting and finance courses), and have two years professional experience in government accounting. The Web site includes information on how to prepare for the CGFM exam and a list of testing centers. To maintain certification government accountants must complete 80 continuing education hours every two years. The Web site at http://www.agacgfm.org also includes a job site where you can post your resume and search for jobs.

In contrast to management accountants, who are part of a corporate executive team, public accountants service multiple clients-corporations, governments, nonprofit organizations, small businesses, or individuals-and perform a variety of functions for those clients. Their services may include consulting on the tax implications of various business decisions and preparation of tax returns, advising on employee compensation and benefits, designing accounting and data-processing systems, and performing external audits of financial records. It is this latter function that can make a public accountant an appealing candidate for a management accounting job. Wouldn't it be great to have someone inside the corporation who knows what the external auditors are looking for? But moving into management accounting is not the only way up for a public accountant. You may opt to move up the ranks in a public accounting firm or start your own accounting firm.

If you loved Agatha Christie as a kid and once wanted to be a detective, public accounting offers something special for you—forensic accounting. Forensic accountants are public accountants who work with police or FBI agents and attorneys to investigate crimes such as securities fraud and embezzlement. You can also investigate fraud and malfeasance as a government accountant, but there are other opportunities in government accounting as well. Some government accountants perform the duties of a management accountant, but for a federal or state government agency instead of a corporation. This may be a good field for you if you want to perform a public service or if you are attracted to the security of a government job. You may wish to rise up within a government agency or use what you have learned about government auditing to land a job for a public company subject to government regulation.

As an accountant you may select a work setting that suits your personal style, from a Fortune 500 corporation or huge accounting firm to your own small business. You can also choose a type of business that interests you. For example, would you like to work in the management accounting department of a glamorous Hollywood movie studio or for a public accounting firm that audits the movie studio? Are you zealous in your commitment to bettering the environment? Although not yet its own field, accountants often evolve to focusing on the cost-benefit of environmental issues. Why not show the company or client for which you work the cost benefits of adopting measures to reduce their carbon footprint? School districts, grocery stores, publishers, pharmaceutical companies, television stations, barbershops-every business needs an accountant.

If you are interested in pursuing a career as an accountant, education and certification will help you land your first job. Most accountants have a bachelor's degree in accounting, finance, or business, and many accountants have a master's degree. It is possible, however, to supplement a bachelor's in another field with finance and accounting courses. Many employers require certification or evidence that you are pursuing certification. The Certified Public Accountant (CPA) designation is preferred by most potential employers or clients and required for any accountant who files reports with the Securities and Exchange Commission (SEC).

If you are in management accounting, your salary may get an added boost if you obtain the Certified Management Accountant (CMA) designation from the Institute of Management Accountants (IMA). Accountants with a CMA earn 25 percent more than non-certified accountants, and those with both the CMA and CPA earn 32 percent more, according to the IMA's Annual Salary Survey in the June 2008 issue of *Strategic Finance* magazine. This certification requires specific educational credentials, professional experience, and passing an exam. Government accountants may find more job opportunities with federal, state, and local agencies if they obtain the Certified Government Financial Manager (CGFM) designation, which is also dependent on an exam as well as education and work experience requirements. Regardless of the branch of accounting you choose, every accountant must be good with numbers and detail oriented. Beyond that, you can create the accounting path that best reflects your interests and desires.

You Are Here

There are many different places for an accountant to land and many ways to get there.

Do you yearn to be an accountant, but not have a bachelor's degree and cannot afford to go back to school full time? Try to find a job as a junior accountant, bookkeeper, or accounting clerk. You can then learn on-the-job, impress your boss, and move up in the company. It is a good idea to pursue your bachelor's in the evening and ultimately obtain your CPA.

Do you have a passion you want to pursue but you need to earn a living as well? Accounting may be the vehicle to pursuing your dream. Remember, every business needs an accountant and even volunteer organizations have expenditures that need to be monitored. Look at non-profit organizations that do the work you believe in.

Navigating the Terrain

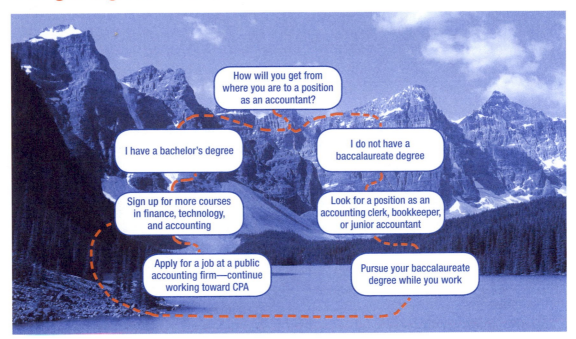

How will you get from where you are to a position as an accountant?

I have a bachelor's degree

I do not have a baccalaureate degree

Sign up for more courses in finance, technology, and accounting

Look for a position as an accounting clerk, bookkeeper, or junior accountant

Apply for a job at a public accounting firm—continue working toward CPA

Pursue your baccalaureate degree while you work

Do you have skills you can transfer to your new field? If you are a former teacher, you might look for a job with the Department of Education in your area or for another organization involved in education. Are you a former nurse? Hospitals and health care organizations need accountants too. Do you have an MBA? You may possess just the right mix to climb the corporate ladder.

Organizing Your Expedition

You will have an exciting journey to find the destination that is just right for you.

Decide on a destination. If you like big firms with thousands of people to get to know and a clear path upward, joining the management accounting team at a Fortune 500 corporation or getting an entry level job at one of the big accounting firms may be the right path. If you like to

Notes from the Field

Tim Davison
Controller / Director of finance, Napolean Art & Productions, Inc.
New York, New York

What were you doing before you became an accountant?

I was about four years into a seven-year lease purchase agreement with two different elderly local farmers. I had a bachelor of science degree in physics and a master's in education. I had intended to pursue an advanced degree, but a family tragedy made it necessary for me to return home to western Oklahoma. That's when I started the farming operation. I had my own farming operation in western Oklahoma.

Why did you decide to become an accountant?

My cash flow from farming was getting progressively worse, and I wanted to find a day job until my farming operation turned around. I was able to get a job as a junior accountant at the local, newly built, privately managed prison. Although my initial decision was one of expediency, not career change, I gradually learned that I liked accounting and was good at it.

What was involved in terms of education/training and getting your first job?

Fortunately I had taken a lot of accounting and finance courses as part of my master's in education. In fact I really had the equivalent of a BS in accounting. That helped me land the junior position at the prison. Over

travel and experience different types of work, seek employment with one of the big accounting firms that have offices around the world. In order to help new accountants find their niche, these firms send them to different destinations and expose them to many different types of accounting, from auditing and tax consulting to budget analysis and business strategy. If you prefer to stay close to home, you may be happiest in a small accounting firm (or maybe ultimately starting your own firm), servicing local businesses and individuals. Finally, if you are passionate about a certain cause, a nonprofit company or an accounting firm that services those companies would be a fine fit.

a five-year period I rose up to become controller for the prison manage-ment company in Nashville, Tennessee. As controller I worked as part of the management team when the company was sold to a competitor and then to a security consulting firm headquartered in New York City. When that company was sold I took a job as controller/director of finance at a small production/post production company that does test commercials for advertising agencies.

What are the keys to success as an accountant?

A rock solid understanding of the accounting process and of the way fi-nancial information is used is essential. Being able to understand what is important and set priorities will take you a long way in the eyes of your superiors. As a management accountant you have to really understand the entire business and be able to look beyond the numbers. Not every decision can or should be based on numbers alone. A public accountant has to have a complete understanding of accounting rules, standards, and procedures. Any accountant has to be good with numbers, of course, and very detail-oriented in terms of recording financial data correctly and completely. You also need to understand computers and database management problems.

To move up you need to have skills not necessarily related to account-ing. People skills are essential for any upper level position. Management skills are vital once you start supervising others. If you want to move up in management accounting you need to become knowledgeable about all aspects of the business.

Scout the terrain. A good resource is the American Institute of Certified Public Accountants (AICPA). Its Web site has a computer game that will help you analyze your personality traits and discover the type of work that would best suit you. The AICPA Web site offers detailed descriptions of the different types of accounting jobs and suggested pathways to the job of your dreams.

Find the path that's right for you. If you are headed toward one of the big accounting firms, make sure you get your degree (or take account-ing and finance courses if you already have a degree) at an accredited university or college. Contact AICPA for a list. Try to get an informational interview early in your quest so that you know exactly what the firm you want is looking for. Look at where these firms have offices, and determine whether or not you will need to relocate. Contact other specialty professional associations, such as the Institute of Management Accountants (IMA), Advancing Government Accountability (AGA), or the Association for Certified Fraud Examiners (ACFE) to find out about local meetings and networking functions.

Landmarks

If you are in your twenties . . . Applying for a job at one of the large public accounting firms will give you a good basis for almost any career path you choose. You will learn from senior accountants and will be exposed to many different types of accounting. After a few years you may decide to continue a career path in public accounting or to use your expertise to market yourself to corporations as a management accountant.

Essential Gear

Certified Fraud Examiner (CFE) credential. The Association of Certified Fraud Examiners (ACFE) offers the CFE credential to those who pass a rigorous four-part test (criminology and ethics, fraudulent financial transactions, fraud investigation, and legal elements of fraud) and meet education and experience requirements. To maintain certification you must maintain high ethical standards and continuing professional education requirements. The Web site at http://www.acfe.com includes information on studying for and taking the exam. It also has a job board. CFEs earn almost 22 percent more than non-certified colleagues, according to the 2008 Compensation Guide for Anti-Fraud Professionals.

If you are in your thirties or forties . . . You might still want to apply for a job at one of the major public accounting firms. Consider beginning your career with one of the many smaller national, regional, and local accounting firms. It is harder, though not impossible, to move up the ladder without some experience performing audits or doing tax work for one of these firms. Alternatively, you might look for a position in a large corporation with a sizeable accounting department. You could start in cost accounting, budgeting, or auditing and gradually rise up in your department.

If you are in your fifties . . . Enhance your marketability by combining your new accounting expertise with expertise from your previous career. Look toward jobs in businesses related to your former field, such as schools if you were a teacher or health facilities if you were a nurse. You might also rely on contacts in your community. Think about starting a small accounting firm to service local stores, businesses, and individuals.

If you are over sixty . . . You might want to zero in on the growing retirement age population. Contact the Accreditation Council for Accountancy and Taxation (ACAT) for information on the Elder Care Specialist (ECS) designation. With expertise in estate and trust planning and financial planning for older Americans you could develop a practice targeted to this population.

Further Resources

The **Association to Advance Collegiate Schools of Business (AACSB International)** lists schools accredited in business and accounting organized according to name or by location. http://www.aacsb.edu/accreditation/AccreditedMembers.asp

The **American Institute of Certified Public Accountants (AICPA)** is your "one-stop shopping" association to guide you in becoming an accountant and landing your first job. You can find a list of accredited schools, possible scholarships, and, when you are ready, a job search section to post your résumé and scan available jobs. http://www.aicpa.org

The **Uniform CPA Examination** qualifications are set by the individual states, but all states require a bachelor's degree and many now require 30 hours of additional coursework. The CPA Exam Web site tells you everything you need to know to prepare for or take the Uniform CPA Exam. http://www.cpa-exam.org

The **Institute of Management Accountants (IMA)** offers the Certified Management Accountant (CMA) designation to candidates who meet education and experience requirements and pass an exam. http://www.imanet.org

The **National Society of Accountants (NSA)**, the professional association for "main street" accounting and tax professionals, offers a range of professional education services and networking to help the solo practitioner or small accounting firm stay current. http://www.nsacct.org

Auditor

Auditor

Career Compasses

Do you have or are you willing to obtain these skills?

Relevant Knowledge of information technology, accounting concepts, and recent changes in business laws and regulations (40%)

Mathematical Skills, financial literacy, and computer skills to calculate risk/benefit, understand accounting issues/controls, and use spreadsheet and electronic work paper software (10%)

Communication Skills to present complicated data to executive staff and to engage colleagues or clients who may feel threatened by you (40%)

Ability to Manage Stress in an environment where every detail must be accurately recorded and people may be resistant to your questions (10%)

Destination: Auditor

Did the recent business scandals make your blood boil? Are you angry at those who ruined corporations, caused employees to lose their jobs, depleted investor returns, and cost taxpayers money? If you yearn to do something to protect companies from fraud, embezzlement, and other malfeasance, or if you want to help companies succeed by creating more cost-effective ways of doing business, you may want to become an auditor. The plethora of recent business scandals—as well as the new legislation to protect against future ones—and the increasing number of new businesses make this a rapidly growing field, according to the Bureau of Labor Statistics. Audits cover a wide range of business functions in addition to financial statements, and people from a wide range of backgrounds can enter this growing profession.

There are two main types of auditors. Internal auditors, who work for a corporation, help their companies run better by assisting in the management of key business risks. They review the development of new systems to ensure they are efficient and cost-effective, and evaluate these systems on an ongoing basis. They aid in setting controls to protect their company from fraud or other wrongdoing, and they periodically search for evidence of such. Auditors may monitor compliance with laws and regulations, assess the efficiency of the production process, evaluate the use of labor and other resources, and verify financial records. They may also monitor other processes specific to the individual business, such as customer satisfaction or manufacturing. In addition to the internal auditing department, public companies must by law submit to an independent, outside audit every year. The external auditors, who evaluate the corporation's financial statements and opine on their accuracy, are CPAs who work for public accounting firms or independent consulting firms.

Essential Gear

Get certified. Certification is very important in this field. "Don't let your certification lapse," cautions Neil Solari of Robert Half International. "Make sure you take the requisite continuing education courses to renew your certification annually," he adds, noting that most employers prefer or even insist on certification. The IIA offers the highly-regarded Certified Internal Auditor (CIA) designation based on meeting educational and experience requirements and passing a stringent examination. ISACA offers the Certified Information Systems Auditor (CISA) designation to those who meet education and experience requirements and pass a multiple-choice examination.

Since information technology is a huge part of almost all businesses today, controls over these systems are evaluated as part of an internal audit, and many internal auditors specialize in information systems. However, according to Anthony Noble, vice president of IT (information technology) Audit at Viacom and member of the Information Systems Audit and Control Association (ISACA) Assurance Committee, "Firms employ three to four times as many financial auditors as IT auditors."

The IT auditor ensures that security and financial controls are built into computer systems; he or she then performs technical audits of these systems to ensure security controls are effectively in place. IT auditors also provide support on operational/financial audits and are involved in special projects, such as fraud investigations.

While the goals of the auditor are laudable—helping the company run more efficiently and protecting it from fraud—not everyone who works with the auditors sees it that way. "It can be a bit depressing," reported one auditor, explaining that no one is ever glad to see you. Whether you are an internal auditor working with your colleagues in other departments or an external auditor coming in from the outside, many staff members will feel you are "snooping around" and bothering them. They are worried that the auditor does not really understand what they do, will come up with unreasonable suggestions to change the way they work, and may even recommend that their jobs be eliminated. That said, even though you will spend a lot of time looking at data, you must have top-notch people skills to be a successful auditor. You need to engage people on staff and put them at ease. You also need excellent communication skills to report your findings and recommendations to your superiors.

If you are doing external financial audits, becoming a CPA (certified public accountant) is very important. The globally recognized certification for internal auditors is the Certified Internal Auditor (CIA) credential, which requires education, experience, character references, and the passing of a stringent four-part exam. If you are working in information technology, the Certified Information Systems Auditor (CISA) designation is recognized worldwide and preferred by many employers. All of these certifications require evidence of continuing education for renewal. Lifelong learning is essential since laws, rules, and regulations are ever-changing and technology is ever-improving.

Essential Gear

Join local chapters of the IIA and ISACA. With membership to these organizations you can begin to network with professional auditors, learn more about their work, and find out what courses or programs will be most useful to you. Both associations provide opportunities for you to network in person at educational conferences and online. The IIA's Member Exchange (ME) is an online networking tool for members only. The ISACA also has listservs where you can ask questions and get advice from experienced professionals.

You Are Here

Start here to chart your course to a career as an auditor.

Do you have a degree in accounting or finance? Working as an external auditor for a public accounting firm will give you the experience you need to apply for an internal auditor position at a corporation. Corporate executives look for internal auditors who understand what external auditors are seeking, and can therefore prepare the company for these outside auditors.

Do you have a degree in computer science, management information systems, or accounting information systems? Experience doing external IT audits for a public accounting firm is a solid background for a corporate job in information systems auditing. Your expertise may get you a job in the IT Audit department of a corporation as well. There is a good chance you will receive on-the-job audit training as you provide technical support to the department.

Navigating the Terrain

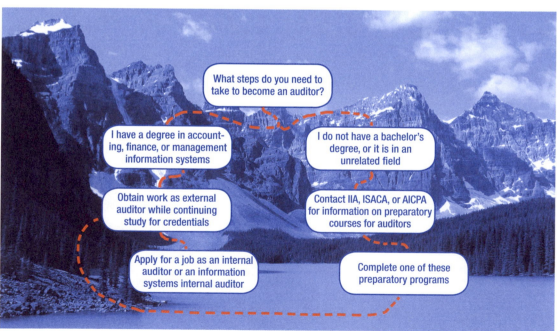

What steps do you need to take to become an auditor?

I have a degree in accounting, finance, or management information systems

I do not have a bachelor's degree, or it is in an unrelated field

Obtain work as external auditor while continuing study for credentials

Contact IIA, ISACA, or AICPA for information on preparatory courses for auditors

Apply for a job as an internal auditor or an information systems internal auditor

Complete one of these preparatory programs

Do you have a degree in a seemingly unrelated field? Think about how your skills may be transferable to a career in auditing. Psychologists may have an advantage in analyzing human behavior and uncovering fraud. The industrial engineer's knowledge of controls is helpful in internal auditing. Public relations experience, which involves crisis/risk management, is also applicable to auditing. Contact the Institute of Internal Auditors (IIA) or ISACA to figure out what additional courses you need and help you segue into an auditing career. If you are in non-auditing job in a corporation, ask your manager if you can be assigned to cross-functional projects with the internal auditors. Talk to the auditors at your corporation to learn more about what they do.

Organizing Your Expedition

Before you set out, know where you are going.

Decide on a destination. What type of work environment is most appealing to you? Only fairly sizeable companies can afford to have auditors on staff. If you want to work as an internal auditor you will have to work for a medium to large size corporation. If you choose to work as an external auditor you might work for a large accounting firm or find a job at a smaller independent auditing firm. Some internal auditors freelance or work independently, particularly in the technology field.

Scout the terrain. Look at the job listings on the Web sites of the IIA and ISACA to see where most jobs are located. You will probably have to live in a fairly big city where there are large businesses in order to find work as an internal auditor. If there are smaller companies in your area you might be able to provide independent technology audit services to them. The big accounting firms have branches in many cities throughout the country.

Find the path that's right for you. "Auditors with a CPA and audit experience at one of the accounting firms can pretty much write their own career ticket in the accounting and finance industry," says Neil Solari, vice president of permanent placement operations at Robert Half International, the first and largest staffing services firm specializing in

Notes from the Field

Anthony Noble
Vice president—IT audit, Viacom, Inc.
New York, New York

What were you doing before you became an information technology auditor?

I was working in IT as a mainframe systems programmer in a large data center for a major brokerage firm. This was a very technical position and the role was focused on keeping the mainframes operating efficiently to ensure stock trades would be performed in a timely manner. It required a lot of weekend and night work as maintenance on the systems could only be performed during non-trading hours and required me to be on call 24/7 in case production problems occurred.

Why did you decide to become an IT auditor?

I was also responsible for installing and maintaining the security software on the mainframe and was subject to internal audits of my work to ensure the brokerage systems were well controlled and secure. I became interested in the work as it required no weekend and night work or to be on call 24/7 to solve production issues. I discussed the job prospects with the IT internal auditor at my company, but no vacancies were available at the time.

What was involved in terms of education/training and getting your first job?

At the brokerage firm I was heavily trained in installing and maintaining the mainframe operating and security system so I had strong information technology experience. I also had a degree in statistics. I did not have a background in auditing, however, except for having been audited in the past. I was lucky to find an IT internal audit position through a

accounting and finance. If you have a degree in accounting or finance, this is an excellent path to a career as an internal auditor. If, on the other hand, you have considerable technology and computer expertise, you may be able to start with the IT compliance group of a major corporation, or in an external IT auditor position at an accounting firm or a firm of IT risk consultants. If you do not qualify for the above, do not despair. Think about whether you can offer a unique perspective to an auditing department.

recruiting firm with a major banking corporation that had several large mainframe data centers and no one technical enough to audit them. They had looked for qualified IT auditors and found none available so they decided to hire technical IT people and train them on the audit side. After they hired me the corporation sent me to several basic auditing classes, and I was mentored by other staff that had the audit experience I lacked. I also took classes at the local ISACA chapter to prepare for the CISA certification exam. I passed the exam on the first try but had to wait another year to obtain the experience required for certification. I feel that having such a strong IT background allowed me to relate the auditing concepts to my past work. I managed a lot of successful data center audits for that corporation around the world.

What are the keys to success as an IT auditor?

A good IT auditor has an understanding of IT risks and controls. Knowledge of accounting concepts is also useful. You have to follow professional guidance, work ethically, and adhere to the ISACA Code of Professional Ethics for ISACA, IIA, or AICPA, depending on your individual certification. A good IT auditor thinks logically, audits with professional skepticism, and is able to identify the IT and business risks in the area being audited and design and execute tests of controls based on risk. When IT auditors identify testing exceptions (such as control design deficiencies and breakdowns in controls), they must be able to assess the exception based on risk and exposure and present the exception both to a technical and non-technical audience. In terms of "soft" skills, IT auditors should be able to develop good working relationships with their clients (internal or external) and the operational/financial auditors with whom they work.

Go back to school. Before you choose a school or decide on any classes, contact one or both professional associations. The IIA and ISACA both have academic relations departments and provide curriculum recommendations to universities. You can look up participating schools or see if any IIA or ISACA courses or seminars will be sufficient. Both associations also have job centers. Scan those to see what employers ask for in terms of degrees and certification. Although most auditors today have a degree in accounting, finance, or management information systems, you may be able to supplement your degree in another field with courses through these professional associations.

Landmarks

If you are in your twenties . . . Go for that accounting or finance degree, followed by a job for one of the top accounting firms. Earn your CPA while you garner three or four years of experience doing external audits. Write your ticket to a job as an internal auditor.

If you are in your thirties or forties . . . You may want to follow the same path or contact one of the professional associations to help you choose courses to prepare you for internal auditing or find a school to earn your degree if you do not have a bachelor's degree. Look around at your current workplace. If there is an auditing department, try to get on cross-functional projects so you can work with the auditors.

If you are in your fifties . . . If you have strong computer skills, try to break in via an IT consulting firm. These firms provide IT services to small businesses that cannot afford a staff IT person. With larger businesses, they may be called in for projects that the staff person cannot handle. The two types of IT consulting firms are professional service firms, which maintain a working staff; and staffing firms, which call in consultants from different places and assign them to projects. There are also people who work independently as IT consultants.

If you are over sixty . . . It will be difficult to break in to this field if you have no background. If you have accounting or information systems expertise, however, an IT staffing firm might be a good way to get started until you feel you can perhaps work as an independent contractor.

Further Resources

The **Institute of Internal Auditors (IIA)** has over 160,000 members in 165 countries. This association can help you figure out what additional education or training you need to become an auditor. This is also the place to find out about the CIA certification and to look for educational conferences and materials.   http://www.theiia.org

ISACA, formerly known as the Information Systems Audit and Control Association, now goes by its acronym to reflect the broad range of IT professionals it serves. This global association sponsors the CISA designation and has a membership of over 86,000 in 70 countries around the world. The Web site includes a list of recommended universities. http://www.isaca.org

Stockbroker

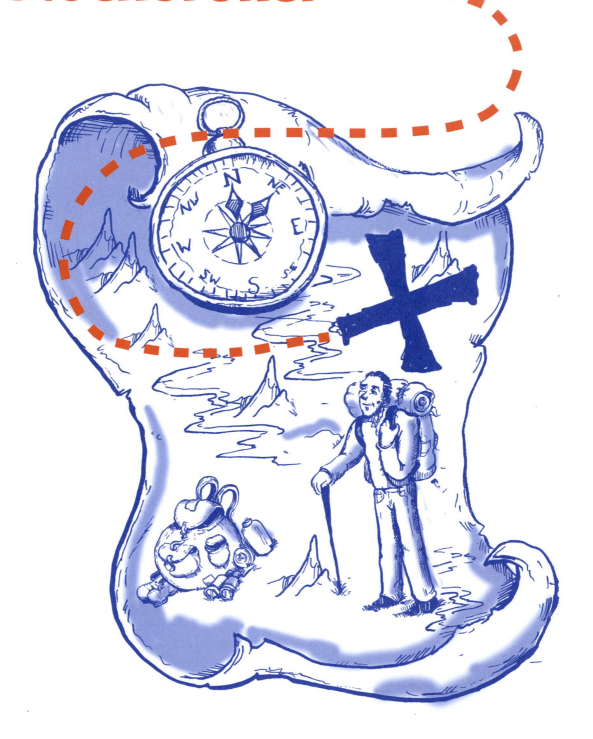

Stockbroker

Career Compasses

If you are high-energy and hardworking, you may want to think about becoming a stockbroker.

Relevant Knowledge of rules and regulations that impact the financial markets (30%)

Mathematical Skills to quickly calculate and analyze costs and ratios (10%)

Communication Skills to attract and maintain clients (30%)

Ability to Manage Stress as the market fluctuates and clients worry (30%)

Destination: Stockbroker

If you are a calm, easy-going person who values peace at work and stability in salary, stop reading and go to the next chapter. A stockbroker's career is one of exhilarating highs and devastating lows. A stockbroker is a salesperson constantly on the lookout for new business. He or she handles others peoples' money and must understand the ever-changing, ever-confusing financial markets. As a stockbroker you can count on long hours and nearly constant stress. There will be heavy competition for jobs and clients. Many people fail soon after starting a career as a stockbroker, but those who succeed can attain heights rarely achievable in other professions. If right now you are feeling enthused rather than deterred, you may have the right personality to pursue a career as a stockbroker.

Stockbrokers sell securities—stocks, bonds, mutual funds and other financial instruments—to individuals and institutions such as businesses and foundations. The broker discusses the pros and cons of a trade with the client before purchasing or selling a particular security. The broker needs to know how the value of the company compares to the current share price and how analysts currently rate the risk of that security. This means the broker needs to fully understand the different securities, how the markets work, and how current economic conditions might impact these securities. Most clients value a broker who can look at their entire portfolio and advise on how different sales or purchases impact that portfolio. For example, will this trade make the client very heavily weighted in foreign stocks? Should the client consider more bonds to balance risk?

Essential Gear

Manage your own stock portfolio. If you have traded stocks independently, make your own portfolio a model portfolio to show prospective employers. Demonstrate how you have balanced international and national holdings and different types of stocks to maximize returns and reflect your personal risk profile. Construct a chart comparing your returns to returns of model portfolios offered by major investment firms.

In order to offer this advice, you must have a solid education in business and finance, understand the financial markets, be up to date on rules and regulations, and know how general economic conditions might impact the market. Most stockbrokers have a bachelor's degree in finance or business, and many ultimately pursue an MBA once they start working. However, brokerage companies have extensive training programs for new brokers, so you still have a good shot at this career if you have a bachelor's degree in another area. You will also learn a lot about the markets as you study for your necessary licensing exams.

You must be sponsored by your employer to apply for the series 7 and series 63 licenses from the Financial Industry Regulatory Authority (FINRA). Most often your employer will provide you with a four to six month training program to help you prepare for these exams. All brokers must pass the series 7 (General Securities Representative) exam, which covers equities, debt, options and derivatives, retirement plans, investment company offerings, and taxes. Most states also require a second exam, either the series 63 (Uniform Securities Agent State Law Exam) or the series 66, which combines the state law exam with the investment advisor exam. Alternatively, those who will be giving investment advice may take the series 65 exam. Your employer can guide you as to what you may need in addition to the series 7.

There are full-service brokerage firms and discount brokerage firms. The fee per trade charged by a full-service stockbroker reflects the firm's investment in financial research and the broker's involvement with the client. In addition to sharing the firm's analysis on stocks with the client, the full-service broker offers investment advice and does a lot of "hand-holding." Since these brokers are generally paid by commission, they spend a lot of time trying to generate new business and maintain active current business. This often means participating in evening and weekend events to expand their social contacts, joining civic organizations, and giving lectures to community groups.

In order to give the broker a steady income, most firms offer a "salary," which is a draw against commission. This salary is based on the minimum amount of commissions brokers are expected to earn. The firms usually offer new brokers a salary as they build their client base. Some brokers also function as investment advisors or financial planners. Although these brokers receive commission for some products, such as annuities or mutual funds, they usually do not receive transaction fees for every trade and are instead compensated with a percentage of assets under management. This more closely aligns their interests with those of their clients since they are not motivated to trade for commission.

Essential Gear

Join an investment club. This is a free way for you to begin to learn the market while you figure out if this is the career for you. In an investment club a small group of people come together monthly to learn and to make investments. Usually members are assigned different equities to research for an upcoming meeting. Once each member presents the research, the group discusses the pros and cons of investing in a particular equity. There is a lot of information on the web about how to start, run, or join an existing investment club. Some useful sites include: http://www.investmentclubhelp.com, http://www.betterinvesting.org, and http://www.fool.com/investmentclub.

Discount brokers charge a much lower fee per trade than full-service brokers because their employers do not provide independent research and the broker has much less involvement with the client. Discount brokers usually offer the client third-party research on their firm's Web site. If you chose to work for a discount broker you will probably work in a large call center with hundreds of other brokers. In some call centers you will make cold calls to potential clients. In others your work will be primarily to answer client questions and execute trades. You will be paid a salary and perhaps a bonus. You may have to rotate the hours you work since most of these centers are open 24 hours a day.

How do you move up as a stockbroker? Once you become a full-service broker, the more you sell, the more money you make. If you show promise, a firm may give you some large institutional accounts to handle in addition to your individual clients. Stockbrokers can move up in a firm to supervise other brokers or head up a branch. If you do well and pass additional licensing exams, you may be able to manage portfolios. Your personal temperament is as important as your knowledge in determining whether or not this is a career for you. As with any sales position, you must have good interpersonal and communication skills to attract and maintain clients, and you must be able to handle rejection and move on. Employers want brokers who seem like aggressive go-getters. Although you do not need to be a sophisticated mathematician, you need to be good and quick with numbers. Since you will live, eat, and breathe the market for many hours each day, you need to be truly interested in it in all its quirks. You need to have high energy to work long hours in a fast-paced environment. As it can be as demoralizing as it is exciting, one must be sure he or she has the right personality before embarking on this career path.

You Are Here

How can you get to a career as a stockbroker from where you are now?

Do you have sales experience in another field, such as real estate or insurance? You are halfway there. At least you know you are good at sales and can handle rejection. (You would not be pursuing this if that were not the case, right?) Now you need to figure out if you have the interest in the financial markets and the temperament to work in this high-stress environment. You can begin by watching investment shows on television, reading financial newspapers and magazines, and maybe joining an investment club. During this phase, finish college in the evening if you do not already have a bachelor's degree. Major in finance or business administration. If you are still interested, use your previous sales success to land a job with a brokerage house that will provide the rest of your investment education. Many brokerage firms covet employees with previous sales experience.

Are you coming from the financial or accounting arena? You already have a lot of the base knowledge you will need. Now you need to find out if you are good at sales. Try to find some opportunities to sell or fundraise (similar skills, and, yes, similar rejection) and see if you like it. Maybe your kid's school wants you to sell greeting cards or an organization you belong to wants you to raise money. Consider getting

Navigating the Terrain

How will you get from where you are to a career as a stockbroker?

I have sales experience and a bachelor's degree

I have a financial background

I want to transition from an unrelated field

Prepare your résumé emphasizing your relevant experience

Look for a part-time or volunteer sales job before you make a decision

Take in lots of financial media to test your appetite and aptitude for the work

Apply for a job at a brokerage firm with on-the-job training and licensing preparation

Take some evening courses in finance or investments

Notes from the Field

Vivian Kaufman
Stockbroker, AXA Financial
New York, New York

What were you doing before you became a stockbroker?

I wanted to pursue a career in psychology. After I got my bachelor's degree I landed a job at the National Institutes of Mental Health. It was the type of job any psych grad would have killed for, so I decided to take it for a year before going back to school for my doctorate. While working at the NIMH I learned that I did not really like the work. I traveled for a year with my soon-to-be husband and then came back to the states and did not know what to do. My husband had two businesses, and he asked me to take over the one that had not been doing well. It was a retail clothing shop. I turned the business around and ran it successfully for over 10 years.

Why did you decide to become a stockbroker?

I found turning around the retail business exciting, so I knew I liked at least some aspect of business. But I was getting bored. I asked every customer who came in to the shop what they did for a living and if they liked it. One day a customer told me about his job at AXA and offered to let me follow him around for a day. He was a stockbroker/financial planner. I went with him and found the work really interesting.

a part-time sales job, explore some volunteer sales opportunities, and begin to take courses in finance.

How will you handle the stress? Think about recent events in your life. How did you handle it that day when you had a presentation due at work, your son broke his arm and you had to rush him to the emergency room, and you got home and your basement was flooded? How did you feel at that meeting when no one agreed with you and no one liked your ideas? Such overwhelming feelings are comparable to the daily dilemmas you may face as a stockbroker.

What was involved in terms of education/training and getting your first job?

Since the attrition rate for brokers is so high, companies like AXA are always on the lookout for new people. They did not pay me, but they put me through all the training courses I needed to prepare for my licensing exams. While I was training I was gradually closing the clothing business and raising my young daughter. Slowly I started to build clientele, mostly from friends and friends of friends. I was 40 years old so I had friends with money to invest. Even though I did not have much experience, they trusted me because they at least knew that I would try to do the right thing for them.

What are the keys to success as a stockbroker?

It is really important to be comfortable with the sales process. You have to find people, meet people, understand what they need, and get them to trust you. I think people can tell if you have a genuine desire to help them. Communication skills are also vital. If you cannot explain your recommendations to someone they will not take them. You also need to be self-motivated and self-directed. No one is going to tell you to get back to work. This is why many of the people who succeed come from careers in sales or from having their own business, such as accountants and lawyers.

Organizing Your Expedition

If you have not been discouraged by the discussion of hard work, long hours, and stress, then it is time to get ready to become a stockbroker.

Decide on a destination. Do you want to begin working for a full or discount brokerage firm? If you have a family or if you are self-supporting, starting out in a discount broker's call center offers you an opportunity to earn a salary while you learn the business.

Scout the terrain. First you must decide if you will need to move and if you want to move. Most stockbrokerage firms are in major financial cities, such as New York, Los Angeles, and Chicago. Look at the job listings on the Web site for the Securities Industry and Financial Markets Association (SIFMA) and check the Web sites for executive search firms and online employment firms that service the financial industry. See where the jobs are located. Once you decide on a location, try to learn as much as you can about the brokerage firms in that area. Scan the Web sites of brokerage and mutual fund companies. Try to meet stockbrokers so you can get the "inside scoop" on different firms. Go to job fairs where you can talk to stockbrokers. Look for meetings in your area at on the FINRA and SIFMA Web sites. Look for firms with good on-the-job training programs and courses to prepare you for the licensing exams.

Find the path that's right for you. If you have a good sales background you may want to focus your attention on firms with good financial training. If you are coming from the financial end, working in a call center for awhile might give you an introduction to the sales experience. Make sure that whichever firm you choose will sponsor and prepare you for the licensing exams.

Landmarks

If you are in your twenties . . . If you have a degree, head for one of the major brokerage firms. You will get a great education and the experience will look good on your résumé.

If you are in your thirties or forties . . . You may very well be at the ideal age to make this transition. Friends of your age are more likely to have money to invest than their younger counterparts. They can provide a great base to help you start your career. See if you can find a place where expertise from your previous career will be useful. For example, perhaps you can specialize in health care stocks or technology stocks if you have experience in one of those areas.

If you are in your fifties . . . This may be a good time for you to focus on the huge baby boom generation. Many middle-aged people find it difficult to trust a young broker. Consider emphasizing estate and retirement planning.

If you are over sixty . . . The high stress factor of the job may make this a difficult field to enter at this point. Consider joining a small firm and focusing on those near or in retirement. Give lectures at community groups and senior centers.

Further Resources

The **Financial Industry Regulatory Authority (FINRA)** provides information on licenses, offers courses to help you prepare for licensing exams, and sponsors conferences and online courses to help you stay current. http://www.finra.org

The **Securities Industry and Financial Markets Association (SIFMA)** has a job site and offers educational conferences and courses. http://www.sifma.org

The **American Academy of Financial Management (AAFM)** is a good source for accredited business schools and educational offerings. http://www.aafm.org

The **American Investment Training Institute** offers courses to help you prepare for the licensing exams. If you take one of their courses and pass the exam, they will help you with your résumé and market you to hundreds of firms.   http://www.aitraining

Brand Manager

Brand Manager

Career Compasses

Find out what it takes to become a successful brand manager.

Relevant Knowledge of your product, the market it will compete in, and technical marketing strategies (40%)

Mathematical Skills to maintain a budget, understand statistics, and calculate pricing (10%)

Communication Skills to educate the market about your product, convince others in the corporation of your strategy, and manage those who report to you (40%)

Ability to Manage Stress as you work long hours under deadline pressure (10%)

Destination: Brand Manager

Fasten your seat belt: You are in the fast lane now. Becoming a brand manager (also called product or marketing manager) is a key stop on the road upward in the corporate world. It is also a great place to take off from if you think you have what it takes to start your own business. But first take a deep breath and relax. There are a few positions you will need to hold in preparation for a brand management career. You will have to first apply for a job as a trainee, assistant, or associate. Once you become a brand manager, however, the road can be very exciting, filled with lessons about people and products, marketing, and managing. Different companies use different titles, but the route up may go something like this: senior brand manager, group brand manager, marketing manager, marketing director, vice president of marketing, and so on. If you show a lot of potential, your company will strategically move you around to positions that give you the broadest perspective on the company, its management, and its products.

Essential Gear

Famaliarize yourelf with The Association of International Product Marketing and Management (AIPMM). This professional association for product managers, product marketing managers, brand managers, and other product professionals, provides numerous educational offerings, including web seminars and conferences. It also publishes *Product Management News and Views*. AIPMM offers certification as a Certified Product Manager or a Certified Product Marketing Manager to those who have appropriate education and work experience and pass an exam. The Web site at http://www.aipmm.com includes a job search database.

What exactly does a brand manager do and why is it so exciting? The brand manager is responsible for everything about the product, but his or her central task is to learn everything about the particular product and the market it will play in. The manager then develops a strategy to make sure the product is profitable and has the best possible position in its marketplace. Part of this is what is called "branding your product." Everything from the name of your product to the consistent images and messages associated with it are designed to create a memorable, highly regarded brand. You also coordinate market research, sales, pricing, manufacturing, distribution, advertising, and public relations.

As you can imagine, this can be very challenging, yet very rewarding, work. Most brand managers work well over the traditional 40-hour week. Evening and weekend work is not uncommon. Although they have an office at the corporation, they travel a lot. If the company is global they may be sent to assignments in other countries. They are expected to visit the company's local offices and customers.

Brand managers need two very different sets of skills. They need technical marketing expertise and excellent management skills. They must be self-motivated and able to work and to lead with little supervision.

Beyond this, brand managers need vision and creativity. John Kaiser, below, notes that "curiosity" is what motivated him to switch careers and to try the many diverse and challenging positions offered at his company. Curiosity and a personality that thrives on change are vital. If you prefer stability and comfort, this probably is not the profession for you. "Problem solving skills are also essential," according to John. Although employment growth is predicted, this is a very competitive market. You will find experienced managers who do not have MBAs, but if you are entering the field now, this advanced degree is almost a prerequisite.

Considering the scandals of the last decade, you may be surprised to learn that marketing success can be accompanied by integrity and a desire to help people. In other words, if you are stimulated by what you have read but concerned about finding meaning, purpose, and decency in marketing, consider the case of pharmaceutical brand manager John Kaiser. When given the choice to work on one of two pharmaceutical products, he says, "I chose the central nervous system (CNS) area because I wanted to help the underdog. That area included psychiatric drugs. There's such a stigma about mental illness, and these people don't have strong advocates like there are for breast cancer and other illnesses." Well, that choice made all the difference. As he developed expertise in the area he was promoted to global marketing director of Prozac, global marketing research director for Prozac and Zyprexa (a schizophrenia drug), global marketing director for an antidepressant in development, and director of neuroscience strategy and new product planning for the company. At the point of early retirement, John was whisked away by a start-up pharmaceutical company with a neurological drug in development and given the title of vice president of strategic marketing and commercial development. "When people ask me what led to my success, I tell them I'd rather focus on significance than success," he notes. "A lot of people have been helped by these products."

Essential Gear

Look into The American Marketing Association. This organization offers extensive educational programs and publications. Their Web site at http://www.marketingpower.com has a job search database and an interactive feature that allows you to contact an expert with your career questions. This association offers the Professional Certified Marketer designation to those who have appropriate credentials and pass an exam. There are local chapters, which may be useful for networking.

You Are Here

How can you break in and get on the path to brand manager?

Do you have a degree? If you do not have your bachelor's, enroll in an accredited business school, full or part time, and study for a bachelor's in business administration. If you already have a bachelor's degree, do not worry if it is in an unrelated field. Just enroll in an MBA program. People still move up through the ranks, but not as often. Working toward your MBA will open many more job possibilities, and MBA programs generally sponsor career fairs for their graduates.

Do you have transferable experience? For example, do you know about technology or medicine or retail products? Arrange informational interviews with human resource people at the companies you target. Find out the best way to break in. Highlight experience on your

Navigating the Terrain

What is your best route to a career as a brand manager?

I have an MBA

I have transferable experience in a product area but do not have an MBA

I do not have transferable experience or an MBA

Visit job and association Web sites and speak with working professionals

Enroll for an MBA, part time or full time

Talk to brand managers to find out if this is the right career path for you

Apply for jobs

Research BBA and MBA programs in your area

résumé that shows you have a unique understanding of products and markets. Let potential employers know if and when you were ever part of their target audience at a previous job. For example, if you are a computer programmer applying for a marketing job with a software company, describe how you evaluate the advantages and disadvantages of different software and how you have used it in the past. Aim for a company with good educational programs in marketing and/or contact the professional marketing associations. Go back to school for your MBA.

Are you switching from an unrelated field? Do a lot of networking to make sure this is the career path you want to follow. Speak to as many people in marketing for different companies as possible. If it feels right to you, work toward your MBA (or bachelor's in business if you do not have a baccalaureate degree). You may want to try to get a corporate job while you are going to school. When you finish your MBA participate in career fairs at your school. If you cannot go for an MBA, speak to headhunters and research companies that provide on-the-job apprentice programs.

Organizing Your Expedition

What route should you follow to become a brand manager?

Decide on a destination. If marketing excites you, that is a great first step. But you will find the work more rewarding and be better at it if you are interested in your product. Look at different companies. Are you most curious about technology? Fashion? Cosmetics? Pharmaceuticals? You may not be able to initially land a job in the company of your dreams, so come up with a few options.

Scout the terrain. Where are the jobs you covet? Review job listings on the professional association sites and on regular job sites. See where the jobs are located. Are you willing to move if there are no choice companies in your area? Keep in mind that this is a career path that often includes relocating, sometimes often, in the course of your career. It is also a path that usually involves a fair amount of travel.

Notes from the Field

John Kaiser
Vice president—strategic marketing and commercial development,
  ACADIA Pharmaceuticals
San Diego, California

What were you doing before you became a brand manager?

I graduated from the University of Cincinnati with a degree in pharmacy. I had worked in both retail and hospital pharmacy during high school and college, and I took a job in retail pharmacy after I graduated.

Why did you decide to become a brand manager?

It was not a one-time decision. It started with curiosity. I met pharmaceutical sales representatives in my pharmacy work and I was curious about what they did. I knew Eli Lilly and Company was a company that offered a lot of opportunities to its sales reps and promoted from within, so I applied to work there. I was happy as a pharmacist, but I was curious about this work. After I worked as a sales rep awhile, Lilly invited me in to what is called an "associate growth or marketing development" program. They rotated me through positions in a few departments—marketing, market research, pricing. It was then that I developed a keen interest in marketing and knew this is what I wanted. I liked being able to develop a brand strategy and then execute the tactical approaches necessary to make it work, to achieve goals. I also saw marketing as a place where I could make a difference and help people. If you market your drug the right way and doctors use it for the right patients, it

Find the path that's right for you. Begin to market your first product, yourself. Look at the companies as the market for your product. What are they looking for? How can you become that product/person? What should you emphasize in your résumé and cover letter? Read the company's advertisement or job description carefully. Try to address their points in your résumé and cover letter. For example, if a company emphasizes leadership and innovation, make sure to highlight and give examples of those skills when you describe your background. Demonstrate you have knowledge of the potential employer's product if you have gained it through a previous job.

can improve those patients' lives tremendously. Marketing your drug the right way means letting doctors know what the drug should and should not be used for. The drug can do harm if it is used incorrectly or in the wrong patient. This really tugged at me. It was a humanistic tug. I also liked problem solving. As a pharmacist I understood the complex science behind the drugs and illnesses, and I liked being able to distill that down to understandable terms without sacrificing scientific accuracy. I know it is easier to see the difference you make it people's lives with pharmaceuticals, but I have to believe that other brand managers feel a sense of satisfaction when their products satisfy the needs of consumers.

What was involved in terms of education/training and getting your first job?

Lilly evaluated me every step of the way as they rotated me through different departments. Once they saw me as someone with potential, they provided me with in-service education courses and they exposed me to different types of work. I really learned through trial and error. I tried things, evaluated the response, refined my approach. Nowadays I think it is much harder to break in if you do not have an MBA. But with or without an MBA you learn from experiences on the job.

What are the keys to success as a brand manager?

The foundation for success includes technical marketing expertise, good problem solving skills, creativity and vision. Leadership skills are essential. You need interpersonal skills to sell your ideas to your superiors, to interface with colleagues and customers, and to manage people who work for you.

Landmarks

If you are in your twenties . . . Finish your undergraduate work, if you have not already done so, work for a year or two, then go back to school for your MBA. Many MBA programs want to know that you have had some experience in the world of business. Try to get a job at a company that has a marketing division, even if you cannot initially land a job in that division.

If you are in your thirties or forties . . . Look at companies with good training programs. Take evening courses toward your MBA. Think about how your expertise can translate into product marketing. If you have technology experience, look at firms that make computers or other devices. If you have medical experience, look at pharmaceutical companies.

If you are in your fifties . . . It may be a bit late to start in this high-pressured, competitive field. Your best shot at breaking in is if you can stress your experience as that company's customer. For example, in writing to a medical device manufacturer, you might say, "During my years as a nurse, I used many different types of intravenous tubing." Demonstrating a working knowledge of the product can go a long way towards a marketing position.

If you are over sixty . . . Similar advice applies to you as those in their fifties. You may be able to identify companies where age is an advantage. Look at companies that create products specifically geared to older consumers, such as denture pastes and senior travel cruises.

Further Resources

Zeromillion provides detailed instructions for writing a product marketing plan.   http://www.zeromillion.com/marketing/templateplan/html
Quick MBA provides a lot of information about product marketing and developing a marketing plan.   http://www.quickmba.com/marketing/plan
KnowThis covers all aspects of brand management from basic marketing principles through strategy, developing a plan, making product decisions, pricing, and distribution.   http://www.knowThis.com

Claims Adjuster

Claims Adjuster

Career Compasses

Determine if you have the right skills to become a successful claims adjuster.

Relevant Knowledge of factors that determine the way a claim is evaluated, such as the cost of construction or auto repair or the number of hospital days for a particular type of surgery (25%)

Communication Skills to deal with clients who may be upset and angry (30%)

Caring about clients who have suffered illness or lost property (25%)

Ability to Manage Stress as you work with people during a difficult time in their lives and search for the fair way to identify and address their claims (20%)

Destination: Claims Adjuster

Becoming a claims adjuster is a logical career switch for people coming from many different backgrounds, particularly those with expertise in health, automotives, building, or law enforcement. Nurses and other health professionals understand medical claims. Auto mechanics can judge what it will cost to get a car moving again. Engineers, architects, builders, and those who have worked in construction have a good sense of what will be needed to put a house hit by a hurricane back on a sturdy foundation. When an adjuster suspects fraud, who makes a better claims investigator than a former law enforcement professional? People with a background in customer service or who have worked in a call center may also be of interest to insurance companies.

You have met or spoken with a claims adjuster if you have ever contested reimbursement from your health insurance company, been in a car accident, or had your home damaged. As a claims adjuster working for an insurance company it is your job to investigate claims (requests for compensation) from insured individuals or businesses. Depending on the situation the claims adjuster may interview the claimant and witnesses (such as in a car accident) and review damage to the car or house. The adjuster goes out to look at and take pictures of the demolished car or storm-struck property. An appraiser is often sent out as well to inspect the car and estimate repair costs. Since so much of the work is "in the field," adjusters often telecommute and may go in to the office a few hours a week or less. In addition to personally assessing damages, adjusters consult professionals—physicians, construction workers, or engineers,

Essential Gear

Take a time management course. Claims adjusters handle several claims simultaneously and they deal with many people in relation to each claim, such as the claimant, witnesses, and consultants. You need an organization system to keep track of details, set schedules, maintain priorities, and help you move from one item to the next. You can find software or online courses on the Web, buy a book such as Julie Morgenstern's *Time Management from the Inside Out*, or buy a system such as Filofax in the stationary store. All systems help you organize your workload, set priorities, and make schedules.

for example—to get a better understanding of damages. Once they have gathered all the relevant information, adjusters prepare a report and offer recommendations about how the claim should be handled. If the adjuster determines that a claim is legitimate, he or she negotiates the settlement with the insured person. If he or she suspects fraud, attorneys and expert witnesses are called in to defend the insurance company's position.

Claims adjusters who work for life or health insurance companies are usually referred to as claims examiners. Instead of going out into the field to look at car or property damage, they work in the insurance company office, look at medical records, and compare the way a patient was treated to preset guidelines. For example, did the patient stay in the hospital longer than the typical appendectomy patient? Was there a reason? The claims examiner might also interview medical specialists. In a life insurance company the claims examiner reviews the cause of death to make sure it is not a cause excluded by the policy. Claims examiners also review life insurance applications to determine if the candidate is too high risk for insurance.

When claims adjusters and examiners suspect fraud, they refer the claim to an insurance investigator. Did the boss set the company's headquarters on fire to collect on the insurance policy? Did the person stage an accident to collect money? Were unnecessary medical treatments prescribed to up the bill? The insurance investigator sleuths around to answer these questions. Interviews, interrogations, and surveillance are the tools of the investigator.

Essential Gear

A laptop and digital camera. These are important tools of the trade for most auto and property claims adjusters. In fact, many claims adjusters spend most of their time at accident sites and transmit photos of damage, personal information, and first-hand accounts to headquarters via the Internet. Software valuation programs then produce cost estimates for repair. Claims adjusters also use their laptops to download forms and files directly from the insurance company's database.

From the type of work they do, you can see that while examiners spend most of their time in an office and work normal business hours, adjusters, appraisers and investigators spend most of their time in the field and often work evenings and weekends. Adjusters, examiners, appraisers, and investigators are usually employed by the insurance company. Some, however, work independently or for consulting firms and are hired by the insurance company on a contractual or project basis. There are also public adjusters who are available for hire by claimants who feel the insurance company is judging them unfairly.

Most people in this field have a bachelor's degree, but it is not impossible to find work with a high school diploma, a vocational degree, or an associate's degree. Auto damage appraisers often complete two-year college programs in auto body repair, which include classes on estimating repair costs. Many insurance companies provide in-house education. The need for licensure varies from state to state, and it is best to check with your state department of insurance, a local branch of an insurance company, or a potential employer about the rules in your state. The value of certification may also vary from company to company.

Employment opportunities for claims adjusters are expected to increase, partially due to growth of the field and partially due to openings created by those who leave or retire, according to the United States Bureau of Labor Statistics. The special appeal of switching careers to become a claims adjuster, examiner, appraiser, or investigator is that the work itself is completely different from that your previous career, but you build upon knowledge you have already gathered. What could be better?

You Are Here

Would you like to become a claims adjuster?

Do you have experience or a degree in auto body repair? Your knowledge can be applied as a claims adjuster or appraiser for automotive damage. Contact appropriate insurance carriers in your area to find out if they will help you make the transition. Ask what type of educational programs they offer. Call your state board of insurance to find out if you need a specific license or if you would be covered under your employer's license.

Do you know something about construction? Maybe you have experience as an architect, engineer, or builder? If so you have the background to work as an adjuster in property damage. To learn the insurance end of this, ask your local insurance company about educational or training programs.

Is your experience unrelated to any area of insurance claims? Many people break into these professions without technical expertise. Contact insurance companies and search job sites to see what types of jobs are available without experience or technical expertise. Pay special attention to customer service jobs. These jobs often require no previous experience, but the experience you gain working with clients can be very helpful when you become a claims adjuster. Consider taking some courses in the area that interests you. For example, if you get a customer service position in a health insurance company, take an evening course in medical billing. This will help you become familiar with medical terms and codes.

Navigating the Terrain

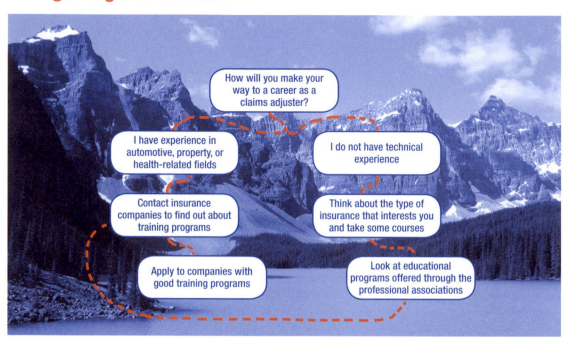

How will you make your way to a career as a claims adjuster?

I have experience in automotive, property, or health-related fields

I do not have technical experience

Contact insurance companies to find out about training programs

Think about the type of insurance that interests you and take some courses

Apply to companies with good training programs

Look at educational programs offered through the professional associations

Organizing Your Expedition

Before you set out, know where you are going.

Decide on a destination. Think about how your experience and expertise can serve you and focus your efforts in that area. Do you want to evaluate auto damage, property loss, or health claims? You need to consider whether you want to work for one of the insurance companies, for an independent consulting firm, or for yourself. The insurance companies usually offer good benefits and training programs. That is a real advantage for your first job in the field. Some independent consulting firms offer salaried positions, but others offer work on a project or contract basis only. While working independently gives you control over your hours and the jobs you take it also involves more income fluctuation. Many claims adjusters who work for or on behalf of insurance companies find the work rewarding and feel that they help people by facilitating reimbursement of valid claims. They also feel they provide a public service by picking up fraudulent claims. If you fancy yourself a crusader, however, and feel great when you are able to help the underdog, you may prefer to work as a public adjuster on behalf of the client.

Scout the terrain. Contact professional associations and attend some of their education/networking functions. Talk to claims adjusters to find out more about what they do and get a sense of the differences between different companies. Ask your insurance agent about these different companies and the pros and cons of dealing with each. In your current job, you may ask people in the human resources department (or other similar department) about their exchanges with local claims adjusters. This can be a productive way of gathering important contacts.

Essential Gear

Become acquainted with Adjusters International. This organization is a disaster recovery consulting organization that focuses on helping clients recover money from insurance claims and FEMA grants. Their Web site at http://www.adjustersinternational.com is a good place to look if you are interested in becoming a public adjuster. Similarly, Adjusters on Call helps residential and commercial property owners achieve a settlement with their insurance company. This is also a good place for information, networking, and possible job opportunities if you are interested in becoming a public adjuster. Find them at http://adjuster-

Find the path that's right for you. Before your actual job search, you can use Insurance-Jobs.com to find out about work in your area. Check the Web sites of insurance companies. These companies usually have a job site, and you can learn about requirements for claims adjusters and examiners in the company.

Landmarks

If you are in your twenties . . . Apply for an entry-level position at an insurance company and take part in whatever educational programs the company offers. If you do not have your bachelor's degree, go back to school full time or part time, depending on your financial needs.

If you are in your thirties or forties . . . Look for an insurance company with a solid training program, or take courses through one of the

Notes from the Field

Kelly Garland
Claims adjuster, Liberty Mutual
Sacramento, California

What were you doing before you became a claims adjuster?

I was working part time for a small stationary store in Sacramento and going to American River College full time.

Why did you decide to become a claims adjuster?

By sheer accident. I had purchased a new truck, and I was so proud that I could buy something on my own. Then, driving home from work one night, I was rear-ended at a stoplight. I reported the claim to my parents' insurance company. A week passed, and I did not hear a word. Back then at the ripe age of 19, I was quite sassy. So I walked into the local Sacramento office, walked right past the reception area, and found my claims adjuster. I told that I could do her job faster than she could. Well, the branch manager for claims was right there, and said to me, "You know we are hiring, let me interview you." I was so mad, I said, "Sure, why not?" I started in clerical for a year until I was promoted to become a first line claims adjuster. I liked the work, liked all the different

professional associations. This is a great time to transition from a field such as nursing, auto repair, architecture/engineering, finance or law. Find the type of insurance that is related to your area of expertise.

If you are in your fifties . . . Consider looking in to claims for the growing long-term care insurance industry. Today many people in their fifties and sixties are buying insurance that will cover expenses for long-term home care, nursing home care, or assisted living, areas not covered by traditional medical insurance policies. Claims adjusters have to determine if the person meets the criteria for reimbursement—generally an inability to perform at least two necessary daily activities, such as bathing or feeding oneself.

cases. The insurance company offered excellent benefits, education reimbursement, on-the-job training, and opportunities for upward mobility.

What was involved in terms of education/training and getting your first job?

I learned a lot while working in clerical and the company provided me with in-service education. It is good to have a college degree, but it is not the end-all to obtain a job as a claims adjuster.

What are the keys to success as a claims adjuster?

You need to be able to handle people who are upset (because they were in an accident or lost a home). Sometimes you become their counselor/shoulder to cry on. If you do not have that patience and ability to handle angry individuals, the job is just not for you. Also, time management is critical. If you are not organized in handling your time, answering calls, returning messages, reviewing claims files to determine coverage, dealing with Department of Insurance regulations, complaints and the like, you will drown. I have seen claims adjusters have mini meltdowns at their desks. Plus you have to figure in the customer service element. Also, you definitely need to have a Type A personality to deal with the challenges of the job. Wilting flowers should not apply.

If you are over sixty . . . You have the best chance if you can capitalize on your area of expertise, such as medical or automotive. Also, seek openings in the long-term care insurance industry.

Further Resources

International Claim Association (ICA) is a good place to start for claims education. ICA offers a Claims Education Program to individuals and companies. This online course is followed by an online exam. Successful completion leads to the designation, Associate Life Health Claims (ALHC), or, for a more advanced curriculum, Fellow Life and Health Claims (FLHC). http://www.claim.org

The American Institute for Chartered Property Casualty Underwriters (AICPCU) and the Insurance Institute of America (IIA) combine to provide excellent educational advice and programs to those working in (or seeking to work in) the field of property damage. You can also earn CPCU certification through their study program and examination. http://www.aicpcu.org

InsuranceJobs.com is the Monster.com for the insurance industry. This is one of the first places to look for job postings nationwide. http://www.insuranceJobs.com

The National Association of Health Underwriters (NAHU) has over 200 chapters nationwide and over 20,000 insurance professional members. This is a good site for information about working for a health insurance company, educational opportunities, and certifications. NAHU produces educational web seminars and provides its local chapters for their educational offerings.   http://www.nahu.org

Bookkeeper

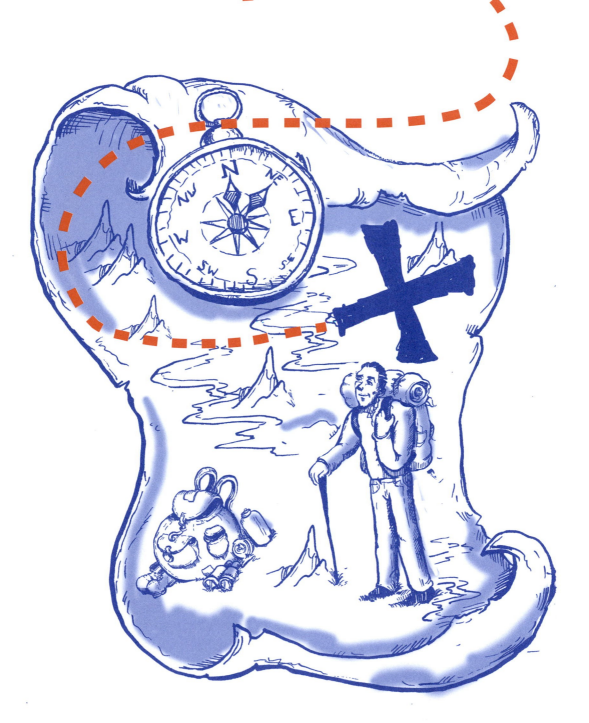

Bookkeeper

Career Compasses

A career in bookkeeping might be just what you are looking for.

Relevant Knowledge of accounting processes (20%)

Organizational Skills to figure out the best way to set up and maintain the company's books (30%)

Mathematical Skills or an aptitude for numbers and some financial literacy (20%)

Communication Skills to elicit the information you need from your boss/client, translate it in to systems that will be most useful, and present it to the accountant (30%)

Destination: Bookkeeper

Bookkeeping offers many opportunities for someone switching careers. This career can be a final destination or a stop along the way. You can work full or part time, for yourself or for a business. You can be part of a bookkeeping department for a large corporation or *the* bookkeeper for a small business. If you have what it takes to be a careful, trustworthy bookkeeper, you can work as much or as little as you want in the work setting of your choice. Many job opportunities are expected for book-keepers over the coming years, according to the Bureau of Labor Statistics. This is due to the large size of the profession, anticipated business growth, and legislation calling for more accurate reporting of financial data by public companies.

Bookkeepers set up (in the case of a new business) and maintain a company's accounting records: debits and credits, accounts payable and receivable, payroll, and profit and loss. They handle transactions, such as writing checks, preparing invoices, and recording payments. They make sure that money that goes out and comes in to the company is properly allocated and recorded. For example, should that check be recorded under expenses or entertainment? The bookkeeper's reports help the management team see how the company is doing and anticipate potential cash flow problems. At year-end, the accountant uses the bookkeeper's records to prepare tax returns.

The bookkeeper is privy to financial information not shared with other employees or with anyone outside the corporation. Trustworthiness is therefore at the top of the list of necessary attributes. You need to be the type

Essential Gear

Get QuickBook. This is the most common accounting software program used today. A great way to learn it is to use it to set up your own business. If you are seeking a job and not starting a bookkeeping business, think of your household as your business. You pay bills, write checks, keep track of income and expenses. Now you can use this as a model to show potential employers or clients.

of person who emanates maturity and seriousness, someone who will not share corporate information with friends on staff or outside. Communication is another essential attribute. Bookkeeper Jo Duer explains that bosses or clients may not be able to directly tell you how they want things done: "You need to talk to them, to find out what their needs are, how they run their business, what information they have to put in, what type of reports they want to see, how they want things broken down." Communication between the bookkeeper and accountant is also crucial. When Jo started her own bookkeeping business she got a lot of referrals from accountants because they knew she made their jobs easier by giving them the data they needed in format they required. Of course bookkeepers have to be comfortable with numbers, and they have to be careful and detail oriented.

The educational background of bookkeepers varies. Almost every employer wants a bookkeeper who finished high school, most want a bookkeeper with some college, and bookkeepers with a two-year associate's degree in accounting are especially marketable. The Certified Bookkeeper (CB) designation from the American Institute of Professional Bookkeepers (AIPB) demonstrates that the bookkeeper has at least two years of relevant experience and has passed a four-part examination. Contact the AIPB for information about preparatory courses for certification. If you have not garnered accounting skills in a previous job or in school, you can work your way up to bookkeeper by taking a clerk type position in the accounting/bookkeeping department of a larger corporation. Most businesses will train you to handle accounts payable or accounts receivable and you can learn more about bookkeeping on the job. If you are in a position where advancement is possible, you should also consider strengthening your position with courses.

Although being a bookkeeper is a great career destination, it can also be used as a stepping-stone. If you want to pursue an accounting career, but cannot go to college full time, you might consider working your way up as a bookkeeper while you study accounting in the evening. If you decide to become a bookkeeper, you will have a career with job security, flexibility, and potential.

You Are Here

How can you start a bookkeeping career?

Is everything about bookkeeping and accounting new to you? Take an adult education or community college basic accounting or bookkeeping class. If you like it and feel you are good at it, you can start to look for a job in the accounting department of a corporation. Look for accounts payable or accounts receivable jobs. Study bookkeeping at night while you get on the job training and impress your bosses during the day.

Do you have some knowledge of bookkeeping from other work you have done? If you already know this is something you will like, go for it. Look for a job in an accounting department (clerical or accounts receivable or accounts payable) and pursue your education part time. If

Navigating the Terrain

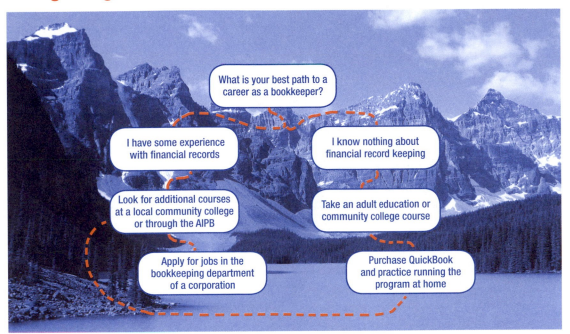

What is your best path to a career as a bookkeeper?

I have some experience with financial records

I know nothing about financial record keeping

Look for additional courses at a local community college or through the AIPB

Take an adult education or community college course

Apply for jobs in the bookkeeping department of a corporation

Purchase QuickBook and practice running the program at home

you are someone who enjoys classroom learning, look for courses at a community college. If you are good with computers and prefer to teach yourself, purchase QuickBook.

Do you have the right personality to be a bookkeeper? You must be careful, thorough, detail-oriented, and good with numbers. In addition you must be mature enough to maintain confidentiality and not share financial information with others. The work is largely solitary, so an ability to be self-directed is crucial.

Organizing Your Expedition

You can structure your bookkeeping career to fit your lifestyle.

Decide on a destination. You have many choices. You can work for a big corporation with a sizeable bookkeeping/accounting staff and lots of on-the-job training, in-service education, and opportunities for advance-

Notes from the Field

Jo Duer
Owner, OutSource Bookkeeping
New York, New York

What were you doing before you became a bookkeeper?

I was a portfolio assistant at an investment firm.

Why did you decide to become a bookkeeper?

My husband (at the time, my boyfriend) had a business with a partner. The partner, who handled the entire financial end, died and my husband did not know anything about the business end. I told him I would take care of it. In my spare time, while I was working as a portfolio assistant, I got him incorporated and set up his books and office systems. I discovered that I loved doing it. I enjoyed setting up a business from scratch.

What was involved in terms of education/training and getting your first job?

I learned QuickBook when I used it to set up his business. It is a great system, very intuitive and fail safe. When I quit my portfolio assistant job, I told the accountants I was leaving and that I was starting my own bookkeeping business. Those accountants became my first clients and they referred others to me.

ment. Or you might prefer a small business where you *are* the bookkeeping department, and you are involved in all aspects of the business. Alternatively, if you have a fair amount of business experience—even if none of it is in finance—you could consider starting your own independent bookkeeping business. Whether you are working for a corporation or for yourself, think about how much you want to work. Will this be a fulltime job or do you want to devote a certain number of hours per week?

Scout the terrain. If you are interested in a corporate career, begin to look at some job search sites, just to see what is available in your area. Every business needs a bookkeeper, whether it is on staff or freelance, so there should be ample opportunities in your area. Also, contact the AIPB and find out about courses in your area, such as community college programs

What are the keys to success as a bookkeeper and as a business owner?

Communication is at the top of the list. You need to draw your clients out and get them to talk about what they want and what they need. They may not be able to articulate what they need and you need to know what to ask to get the important information. You need to understand how they run their business, what information they want to put in, what they want to get out, what type of reports they want to see. You need to know how they want things broken down. Communication with the accountant is just as vital. I keep getting referrals because I make sure the reports I turn out at the end of the year are just what the accountant needs. It is my job to make the accountant's job easier. Flexibility is also important. I look at each client, at each business, as an individual. Everyone wants something a little different and it is my job to meet those needs and to be flexible as those needs change. Of course computer skills are vital. I love QuickBook. Being trustworthy really tops the list because people are sharing very private information. I also like to educate my clients. I help them understand what I am doing.

or other programs for certification. Even if you do not pursue certification, the courses will provide you with knowledge you need. Meanwhile, begin to teach yourself QuickBook.

Find the path that's right for you. If you are relatively young and inexperienced, you may want to start in the bookkeeping department of a corporation while you take evening courses. Begin a job search with the AIPB Web site, look into search firms with substantial financial arms such as Robert Half International, check the classifieds in your local newspaper, and look at other job sites on the web. If you want to look in to starting your own business, start with your accountant. Ask for referrals. Contact small local stores and businesses to see if they need any bookkeeping assistance.

Landmarks

If you are in your twenties . . . Check with the AIPB about educational offerings. Get an associate's degree in accounting/bookkeeping or take courses for AIPB certification. Look for a job in a fairly large corporation so you can benefit from on-the-job training and advancement.

Essential Gear

Network with accountants. Whether you are looking for a job or clients, accountants have the contacts. Once they see how well you keep financial records, they will want you to work on their accounts. They will see you as someone who makes their job easier. Get names of accountants from friends. Ask your own accountant for names of colleagues. Look into the job placement site at the American Institute of Certified Public Accountants (AICPA). Check local AICPA chapters for meetings at which you may network.

If you are in your thirties or forties . . . You may want to look for accounts payable or accounts receivable job while you take evening courses in accounting/bookkeeping. Look for a corporate job, large or small, to get some experience. Once you have some work experience, you may want to teach yourself QuickBook. You can then look for corporate jobs where this system is used, or start your own business.

If you are in your fifties . . . At this stage in your career trajectory, starting your own business may be the way to go. Teach yourself QuickBook. Try to get referrals from the accountants you know. Contact local stores and businesses who may need assistance keeping books. Use your QuickBook model business to show them what you can do.

If you are over sixty . . . The recommendations for the fifty year-olds apply to you as well. In addition to small businesses, you may want to look for individual clients among older people who can no longer maintain their own financial records, but who are more likely to entrust this information with a peer of similar age.

Further Resources

American Institute of Professional Bookkeepers (AIPB), the professional association for bookkeepers, sponsors educational programs, has a chat room and runs a job site. You can find out about courses to prepare for certification.   http://aipb.org

Robert Half International is a search firm with many bookkeeping jobs. http://www.rhi.org

The **Institute of Certified Bookkeepers** is a membership society aimed at promoting bookkeeping, disseminating useful tools and information of the trade, and helping bookkeepers network worldwide. http://www.book-keepers.org

Insurance Underwriter

Insurance Underwriter

Career Compasses

Is a career as an insurance underwriter right for you?

Relevant Knowledge of the different policies offered by your company (25%)

Organizational Skills to handle many details on many applications simultaneously (30%)

Mathematical Skills to understand statistical analyses of risk (25%)

Communication Skills to work with agents, clients, and managers (20%)

Destination: Insurance Underwriter

Ever wonder how the companies decide whether or not to insure you or how much to charge you in premiums? It all comes down to recommendations from insurance underwriters. Insurance underwriters try to rock carefully in the center of the seesaw. It is their job to protect the insurance company from financial loss. They do not want to insure someone at high risk or not charge adequate premiums to cover that risk. On the other hand, they are in business to insure people, and if they do not, their competitors will.

Insurance underwriters analyze data from the insurance application to determine the level of risk. If you are dealing with health insurance or life insurance, you may also get information from physicians and check medical records. You must look for factors that will influence how much medical care the applicant may need in the near future, or determine their risk of death. You are considering factors like age, smoking history, weight, current or past illnesses, family history of illness, and so on. If you are dealing with life insurance, actuarial tables will help you. If you are dealing with casualty or property insurance, you are looking at the location of the property (for instance, if it is in an area prone to flooding) and any safeguards the owner is taking or not taking to protect it. If you are providing mortgage insurance you are evaluating the likelihood that the client will be able to make payments for the term of the mortgage. When you have completed your analysis you decide whether or not to insure

Essential Gear

Know the vocabulary of the job. You can get a glossary of insurance-related terms from the Insurance Information Institute (III) Web site. If you are being interviewed to underwrite life insurance policies, you will want to know that "accelerated death benefits" have nothing to do with how soon the policy holder dies, but rather with the option of collecting benefits during a terminal illness. If you are interviewing for a position in automotive insurance, you should know that "car year" does not relate to the make and model but is the standard measure for car insurance and equals 365 days of insured coverage for a car. Anyone discussing health insurance with a potential employer will want to understand "waiting period" or "elimination period": this is the time from the date of the policy to the date when benefits will be payable. On any interview you will want to know that an "actuary" is a professional skilled in analysis, evaluation, and management of statistical data, and that "rate" refers to the cost of insurance and is usually written per $1,000.00. The III Web site also provides a list of insurance companies and job opportunities organized by state.

the person. If you are going to offer an insurance policy, you write the policy including specifications that address the risk. You also calculate premiums based on the level of risk.

Most underwriters specialize in one of the four main areas of insurance: life, health, mortgage, or property and casualty. Nowadays, more and more companies are offering long-term care insurance policies, and this is becoming a very popular area of specialization. Long-term care insurance is geared to senior citizens and it essentially picks up where regular health insurance or Medicare leave off. Long-term care policies usually provide coverage for home care, nursing homes, and assisted living, often for a period of two to five years. Technology also plays a big part in the work of underwriters today. Software called "smart systems" helps analyze risk and recommends appropriate premiums. The Internet helps underwriters track down relevant information, such as previous instances of flooding or fire in the area around a property in question.

Most underwriters have a bachelor's degree in business, finance, or accounting. There are, however, opportunities to work your way up in many insurance companies. Starting at a lower level while you complete your degree is a good way to break in to this field. Many underwriters begin work as trainees or assistant underwriters, helping to collect information on applicants, but you can start any place in the insurance company. Since so much of the analysis and research is done via computer, excellent computer skills are as important as a degree. Employers are also looking for certain personal characteristics, including people who are detail-oriented, like to analyze data, and have common sense. Interpersonal skills are also valued because underwriters have to deal with agents, other insurance professionals, and sometimes clients.

Essential Gear

Explore various organizations. The American Institute for Chartered Property Casualty Underwriters (AICPCU) and the Insurance Institute of America (IIA) are not-for-profit organizations offering knowledge solutions and professional development services to the risk management and property-casualty insurance community. The Institutes offer the CPCU designation program as well as associate designation programs in areas such as claims, risk management, underwriting, and reinsurance. There are excellent educational programs for those working in (or seeking to work in) the field of property damage. Find their Web site at http://www.aicpcu.org.

The Insurance Institute of America (IIA) offers a training program for beginning underwriters. Certification can also help you in the job market.

The IIA offers the Associate in Commercial Underwriting (ACU) and the Associate in Personal Insurance (API). Both certifications require completing a course of study and passing an exam. Renewal requires evidence of continuing education. The American Institute for Chartered Property Casualty Underwriters offer the Chartered Property and Casualty Underwriter (CPCU) designation to those who pass eight exams, have three years of experience, and agree to abide by a code of ethics. The American College offers the Chartered Life Underwriter (CLU) and Registered Health Underwriter (RHU) designations for life and health insurance underwriters. Both designations also require that you pass exams and have evidence of experience. Underwriters may advance by moving up in the insurance company. Rather than move up, some choose to increase earning potential by becoming agents or brokers. Former underwriters can make especially valuable agents because they can tell clients what to expect, their likelihood of acceptance, and so forth.

You Are Here

Start here to find your way to a career as an insurance underwriter.

Do you work in finance? Your skills are transferable to a career as an insurance underwriter. Highlight your work history on your résumé. Analytical skills are important but so is experience doing careful, detail oriented work, such as bookkeeping.

Do you have technical experience in an area of insurance? Nurses and other health professionals have a big advantage underwriting health insurance policies. Land assessors, construction engineers, real estate agents and surveyors, and others involved in building bring valuable insights to property and casualty work. Contact insurance companies that interest you and ask them how to proceed. Some companies may want you to take a course, while others may provide on-the-job training.

Do you have a clerical background? Your attention to detail and history of careful, methodical work is a benefit. Try to get a job in the underwriting department of an insurance company, if possible. If nothing is available, take another job and let your manager and human resources know of your hope to transfer.

Navigating the Terrain

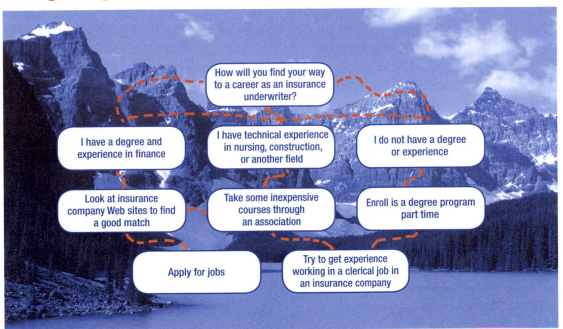

How will you find your way to a career as an insurance underwriter?

I have a degree and experience in finance

I have technical experience in nursing, construction, or another field

I do not have a degree or experience

Look at insurance company Web sites to find a good match

Take some inexpensive courses through an association

Enroll is a degree program part time

Apply for jobs

Try to get experience working in a clerical job in an insurance company

Organizing Your Expedition

Are you ready to get started on your path to becoming an insurance underwriter?

Decide on a destination. You may want to pursue jobs in your area of interest or expertise: life, health, property and casualty, mortgage or the newer area of long-term care. If you do not feel strongly or have experience in one of these areas then you can make yourself open to whatever interesting position becomes available first.

Scout the terrain. Go to the Insurance Information Institute Web site and get a list of insurance companies in your area. Look at the Web sites of companies that interest you. Take a look at InsuranceJobs.com to see what is available in different parts of the country. Meanwhile talk to insurance underwriters about their work. Ask your insurance agent to put you in touch with an underwriter. Contact the local chapter of the professional associations.

Notes from the Field
Susan Kearney, CPCU, ARM, AAI, AU
Senior director of knowledge resources, American Institute
for CPCU/Solidus Insurance Institute of America
Malvern, Pennsylvania

What were you doing before you became an insurance underwriter?

Before I became a property and casualty (P&C) insurance underwriter, I worked in the area of risk management (still within the "insurance" umbrella). My risk management positions included working in a corporate risk management department for a large service company, and subsequently in risk management consulting for a self-insured TPA (third-party administrator).

Why did you decide to become an insurance underwriter?

I was approached by an MGA (managing general agency) regarding a risk management position within their company. While interviewing, I was introduced to the VP of Underwriting who introduced me to the world of underwriting—gave me the big picture and day-to-day responsibilities of an underwriter. Although I was offered a higher-level risk management position, I turned it down and asked if they had an opening in the underwriting department. With my background in risk management and undergraduate degree in actuarial science and insurance, I felt I had enough experience to be an effective underwriter. I got the job, and within one year was promoted to program underwriter and manager of a $25 million book of business in the property/casualty niche business.

Find the path that's right for you. Are there insurance companies in your area? Most underwriters work out of the company's headquarters. However, property and casualty underwriters often work out of branch offices. If you would like to work in property and casualty insurance consider whether you would prefer to underwrite commercial or personal insurance plans. If you underwrite business insurance, you have to evaluate the company's operation fully to ascertain how much coverage is needed. If you choose to underwrite personal property and casualty policies, you may want to specialize in fire, homeowner, workers' compensation, liability, automobile, or marine policies. If you prefer to work for a health or life insurance company you may have the opportunity

What was involved in terms of education/training and getting your first job?

I had an actuarial degree from Temple University that was instrumental in getting my first job. I was actually offered several positions even before graduation so I had no "working" experience. After landing my first job, I also continued my studies and received a master's degree in risk management, as well as pursued professional insurance designations offered through the Institutes' such as the CPCU and ARM. This coupled with on-the-job training, determination, and solid work ethic, provided me a variety of quality positions and promotions throughout my career.

What are the keys to success as an underwriter?

The keys to success as a property/casualty underwriter include the following:

1. Technical knowledge—risk analysis, financial analysis, coverage, systems
2. Solid interpersonal skills including relationship building, ability to work in a team environment, and ability to communicate (verbal and written)—be responsive
3. Sound decision making skills
4. Continuing professional development, and keeping current with trends, changes in industry, products, coverages, and legal.
5. Work with integrity
6. Ability to multitask and meet deadlines

to underwrite group policies. With group polices you will be evaluating the risks of each person in the group to determine the overall risk of the group. For example, the average age of employees in a corporation may impact the overall risk in a group health or life insurance policy.

Go back to school. Most underwriters have a bachelor' degree in finance, business or a related field. It is possible to promote from within if you do not have a degree, but it is a good idea to take evening courses toward your degree while you are working. Alternatively, you may want to take an underwriting course through one of the professional associations or study for certification.

Landmarks

If you are in your twenties . . . Go for the degrees. If you need income, try to get any job you can at an insurance company while you go to school in the evening. Finish your bachelor's degree and go for a master's degree in a finance-related field.

If you are in your thirties or forties . . . Try to get a job at an insurance company while you pursue your degree. Let management know your goal is underwriting and you would like to be transferred to that department. If you have experience in the "content" part of underwriting (such as nursing for health underwriting or engineering for property and casualty under-writing) try to get informational interviews at insurance companies and ask them how to break in. You may be able to get an assistant level posi-tion and learn underwriting on-the-job or they may suggest a course.

If you are in your fifties . . . You may want to look in to the growing field of long-term care insurance. Most people purchase these policies when they are in their fifties or sixties. Sometimes underwriters go on sales calls with agents, and potential clients usually feel more comfortable discussing their cares and concerns with someone in their age group. Although your estimate of risk will be based on specific criteria, such as whether or not the individual has high blood pressure or diabetes, your understanding of the age group can help you understand the issues.

If you are over sixty . . . Your previous experience may make you espe-cially appealing to companies providing long-term care insurance. For example, medical knowledge is helpful in understanding risk factors.

Further Resources

The **National Association of Health Underwriters (NAHU)** has over 200 chapters nationwide and over 20,000 insurance professional mem-bers. This is a good site for information about working for a health insur-ance company, educational opportunities, and certifications. http://www.nahu.org

The **Insurance Information Institute (III)** offers extensive information about how the insurance industry works.   http://www.iii.org

Loan Officer

Loan Officer

Career Compasses

Are you interested in working as a loan officer?

Relevant Knowledge of the current economic situation, market conditions, and rules and regulations covering lending (25%)

Organization Skills to manage multiple loans at the same time (20%)

Mathematical Skills to analyze financial statements (25%)

Communication Skills to interact with clients and executives on the loan committee (30%)

Destination: Loan Officer

Career opportunities for loan officers range from making loans to your neighbors in a small town bank to financing a multinational corporation to solving a country's trade crisis. You have to apply the same principles, the same analysis, and the same skills to your work whether you are contemplating a $6,000 home equity loan or a $40 million mortgage for a building. But where you work, where you travel, the stress level, and how much you earn will vary along with the type of work you do.

You can understand what the loan officer does by remembering what they did *not* do during the banking collapses of 2008 and 2009. Under orders form the top, of course, many loan officers approved loans to people and businesses that could not demonstrate an adequate ability to repay. When scores of people and businesses started defaulting on their loans, the banks collapsed. "We used to sit there shaking our heads," says Cynthia Wang, vice president of Apple Bank, one of the surviving institutions. "We would turn people away knowing they did not have the resources to make payments and then we would see them getting a loan from one of our competitors. We would lose business because our competitors would offer much better terms than we felt were prudent." As the competitors collapsed, the Apple loan officers became very busy again. What did Apple do differently from the banks that failed? Their loan officers applied stringent criteria to determining eligibility and carefully evaluated loan applicants.

The most important part of the loan officer's job is evaluating the applicant's ability to repay the loan. For small loans and individual mortgages, a simple credit check provides a lot of information and reviewing tax returns is pretty straightforward. For commercial or business loans this involves financial analysis and "kicking the tires," according to Cynthia. She explains that after you review the financial statements, you have to see if they make sense in the real world. For commercial lending that may mean knowing the company's product and management and how it fares in the marketplace. For a mortgage, that means looking at the property. Cynthia tells about a recent applicant seeking a mortgage on a building. She visited the building and found there was no boiler. The tenant explained that because his business, a deli, used steam tables there was never any need for heat so he removed the boiler and made better use of the space. "Well that was reasonable in terms of his business," explains Cynthia, "but I asked the building owner, 'how will you replace that tenant if he leaves or goes out of business?' You'll

Essential Gear

Consider getting certified. Although certification has not been the norm in the lending industry, it has become more important in light of the predatory lending practices uncovered in 2008-09. Check out the Loan Review Certificate Program offered by the Bank Administration Institute and the Certified Mortgage Banker (CMB) designation offered by the Mortgage Bankers Association.

have to put in a new boiler to get a new tenant?'" The terms of his loan would have to reflect that possible added expense.

The difference between banks that failed and those that survived rested partially on the way they compensated their loan officers. As this book goes to press, it is probably pretty safe to assume that if you enter this field, you will be paid a salary and perhaps a bonus. The failed banks paid loan officers huge commissions on individual loans. At the surviving Apple Bank and other prudent institutions, loan officers received a salary, perhaps with a bonus. But they were not rewarded for individual loans, and they were not penalized when they did not make a loan. These are undoubtedly the new standard operating procedures of the field.

Essential Gear

Learn a second language and culture. You will be much more marketable if you are fairly fluent in another language and know something about that culture. Many local banks service people who do not speak English. If you decide to go in to commercial lending, you will be operating in a global arena. Fluidity of movement through all levels of that arena is essential to build trust, gain clients, and complete lending transactions.

While one side of the coin is financial analysis, the other side of the loan officer's job is sales: recruiting potential borrowers. Mortgage loan officers try to develop relationships with real estate agents. Commercial loan officers may contact local businesses. Recruitment of individuals for mortgages or home equity loans is usually done through bank advertising.

Most loan officers work for banks or credit unions. Depending on the type of loans you are handling, there may be travel involved. In rural areas, the bank's branch manager may double as the loan officer. As you move toward more populated suburban areas and rural areas, you will find separate lending departments.

The educational paths of loan officers can vary. Many have at least a bachelor's degree in finance, economics or business. In neighborhood banks, it may be possible to be promoted to loan officer from within in the absence of a degree. An MBA or master's in a finance related field is advantageous if you want to work on sizeable commercial or real estate accounts. Becoming a loan officer will open up a range of possibilities. From the quiet of your local bank to the hustle of New York's financial center, there are many career opportunities for loan officers.

You Are Here

Before all else, design your path to a career as a loan officer.

Do you have a bachelor's or master's degree in finance or business? You are ready to look for a job. Think about the type of work you prefer-individual, corporate or commercial real estate-and start to look at job listings. Check out "LenderCareers" on the Mortgage Bankers Association Web site. If you do not have a master's degree, consider pursuing one part time while you are working. If you do not have a degree in business or finance, look for a job at your local bank. Customer service can be a good stepping stone to the lending area. Begin to take evening courses toward your BBA.

Are you able to synthesize large amounts of information? Consider whether or not you are someone who can keep many details in your head and then cut through those details to see the big picture. Although loan

Navigating the Terrain

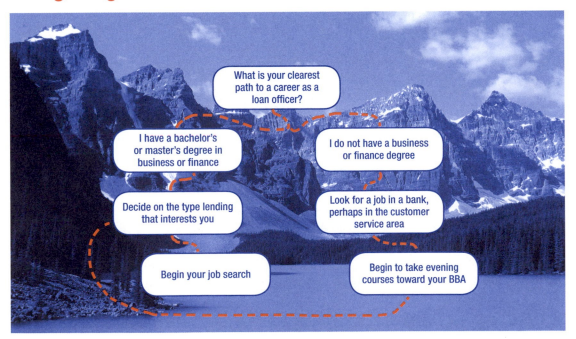

What is your clearest path to a career as a loan officer?

I have a bachelor's or master's degree in business or finance

I do not have a business or finance degree

Decide on the type lending that interests you

Look for a job in a bank, perhaps in the customer service area

Begin your job search

Begin to take evening courses toward your BBA

officers handling personal mortgages generally work with a check list of criteria, those handling larger commercial loans or mortgages have to scrutinize the business and/or property carefully, pull all that information together, and then assess overall risk of default.

Do you have an adequate understanding of the housing market or the commercial real estate market, and are you a good business analyst? If you want to handle personal or business mortgages you need to understand and keep track of all the factors that can influence property value, such as changes in the overall economy and development in the community. You also need to be able to analyze financial data and understand other factors that may impact a business, such as new competition, changes in laws and regulations, shifts in the economy, and so forth. You need to be able to look beyond the numbers and beneath the surface and consider sometimes obscure factors that may impact a corporation's ability to repay a loan.

Organizing Your Expedition

Would you like to provide loans to people like yourself or to multinational corporations?

Decide on a destination. Most loan officers work for banks or credit unions. Do you want to work at your local bank and help your neighbors get mortgages or home equity loans? Or are you headed for a big city and a job evaluating a corporation's ability to repay a loan or a mortgage? In addition to deciding where you want to live, you need to think about the type of work. If you are working with individuals, the loan evaluation process is more straightforward. You can perform a credit check online and review the applicant's tax returns. Also, individual loans for a local bank require a fairly standard report with a recommendation about the loan. If you want to handle huge corporate loans or mortgages, you will be doing the work of a financial analyst described in the first chapter. You will have to do a much more thorough investigation of the company that will involve looking closely at financial records and then stepping back to see the big picture. Corporate loans or commercial mortgages require a much more detailed report submitted to a loan committee. You must present yourself to his committee to explain your recommendations.

Scout the terrain. Talk to loan officers. Go to banks in your area. Contact the professional associations and attend networking functions. Try to get a sense of how different types of loan officers spend their days. Look at job listings on the Web and in your local paper.

Find the path that's right for you. If you want to work for a neighborhood bank, why not try to get a job now, even if you do not yet have the credentials? Look for non-degree jobs in customer service. You will be learning the business and have an opportunity to move up while you pursue your education. If you are headed for a major commercial bank in a big city, try to get some experience before you undertake the move. If you need to complete a BBA or MBA program, ask about job fairs sponsored by the university for new graduates.

Go back to school. The appealing aspect of this career path is that you can start to accrue experience and make contacts before completing your degree. Working in a bank will give you an idea of what loan officers do, even if you are not doing that work yourself. Also most business degree programs want you to have work experience. Many MBA programs encourage or insist on at least a year or two of work experience between getting a bachelor's and entering an MBA program.

Landmarks

If you are in your twenties . . . Complete your bachelor's degree if you have not done so already. Then work for a year or two, preferably at a bank, before enrolling in a master's degree program. Take summer internships at banks during your MBA studies and participate in the career fairs the school sponsors for its graduates.

If you are in your thirties or forties . . . You may follow the advice above if you are interested in commercial lending. However, if you want to work with individuals, this is a great time to contact your local banks. You may be able to generate business for the bank by approaching other people your age who are house hunting. If you have experience in a related area, you may be able to transfer within an institution or use your experience to get a loan officer position. Experience as a financial analyst, auditor, or accountant would make you appealing to an employer.

Notes from the Field

Cynthia Wang
Vice president, Apple Bank
New York, New York

What were you doing before you became a loan officer?

I was teaching art history at the School of Visual Arts.

Why did you decide to become a loan officer?

It was a several-step decision. First I realized that I would never earn enough money to live in New York as an art history teacher. Just being in New York made me think about business and so I decided to go for an MBA at Columbia. While there I realized that I really liked the nuts and bolts courses like finance and accounting, and I did not like the "soft" courses like marketing and managerial behavior. I loved studying the finances of companies to determine whether or not the stock was properly valued. These preferences made me think of loan officer or financial analyst.

What was involved in terms of education/training and getting your first job?

I worked at Chemical Bank (now JP Morgan Chase) during the summer as a business school intern. Prior to graduation Columbia arranged for a lot of potential employers to come in and interview students. I signed up for a bunch of interviews to get a sense of what I might like. I de-

If you are in your fifties . . . Your local bank (or local banks in your area) may be a good place to start. You may want to focus on bringing in clients who need loans for their children's college education.

If you are over sixty . . . Talk to your local bank about working with retired people who may be moving in to smaller quarters and are thinking of refinancing their mortgage. These clients are more apt to trust someone their own age, who has perhaps been through a similar experience.

cided to take a job with Chemical. Since I had studied Asian languages, and I am Asian, both the bank and I thought I would be of value in the international lending area with a focus on Asia. Chemical also put me through a training program. At the time most banks had two training programs, one for those with a BBA and an accelerated program for MBAs. Shortly after I started, they sent me to Taiwan for six months. I was doing analysis of multinational companies. I had to learn about many different industries because in order to make each loan I had to understand that company in the context of the industry and the countries in which it operated.

What are the keys to success as a loan officer?

You need to have common sense, know what is reasonable. If someone presents you with numbers, you cannot take it at face value. You need to look behind the numbers and see if they make sense in the broader market. They say people have three sets of books: the real ones, the ones they show the IRS where they bloat their expenses, and the ones they show the bank where they minimize their expenses. Sometimes people honestly overestimate their projections and sometimes there is outright fraud. You need to be a bit of a detective. You need to know your client. It is really a combination of accounting skill to analyze the finances and an ability to look beyond the obvious, to investigate and to exercise good judgment.

Further Resources

The **Bank Administration Institute (BAI)** has many educational offerings including on-site conferences and webinars. The BAI also offers the course and exam leading to the Loan Review Certificate.
http://www.bai.org

The **Mortgage Bankers Association (MBA)** also has many educational offerings, including courses for the Certified Mortgage Banker (CMB) designation. MBA has a job site called LenderCareers.
http://www.mbaa.org

Appendix A

Going Solo: Starting Your Own Business

Starting your own business can be very rewarding—not only in terms of potential financial success, but also in the pleasure derived from building something from the ground up, contributing to the community, being your own boss, and feeling reasonably in control of your fate. However, business ownership carries its own obligations—both in terms of long hours of hard work and new financial and legal responsibilities. If you succeed in growing your business, your responsibilities only increase. Many new business owners come in expecting freedom only to find themselves chained tighter to their desks than ever before. Still, many business owners find greater satisfaction in their career paths than do workers employed by others.

The Internet has also changed the playing field for small business owners, making it easier than ever before to strike out on your own. While small mom-and-pop businesses such as hairdressers and grocery stores have always been part of the economic landscape, the Internet has made reaching and marketing to a niche easier and more profitable. This has made possible a boom in *microbusinesses*. Generally, a microbusiness is considered to have under ten employees. A microbusiness is also sometimes called a *SOHO* for "small office/home office."

The following appendix is intended to explain, in general terms, the steps in launching a small business, no matter whether it is selling your Web-design services or opening a pizzeria with business partners. It will also point out some of the things you will need to bear in mind. Remember also that the particular obligations of your municipality, state, province, or country may vary, and that this is by no means a substitute for doing your own legwork. Further suggested reading is listed at the end.

Crafting a Business Plan

It has often been said that success is 1 percent inspiration and 99 percent perspiration. However, the interface between the two can often be hard to achieve. The first step to taking your idea and making it reality is constructing a viable *business plan*. The purpose of a business plan is to think things all the way through, to make sure your ideas really are profitable, and to figure out the "who, what, when, where, why, and how" of your business. It fills in the details for three areas: your goals, why you think they are attainable, and how you plan to get to there. "You need to know where you're going before you take that first step," says Drew Curtis, successful Internet entrepreneur and founder of the popular newsfilter Fark.com.

Take care in writing your business plan. Generally, these documents contain several parts: An *executive summary* stating the essence of the plan; a *market summary* explaining how a need exists for the product and service you will supply and giving an idea of potential profitability by comparing your business to similar organizations; a *company description* which includes your products and services, why you think your organization will succeed, and any special advantages you have, as well as a description of *organization* and *management*; and your *marketing and sales strategy*. This last item should include market highlights and demographic information and trends that relate to your proposal. Also include a *funding request* for the amount of start-up capital you will need. This is supported by a section on *financials*, or the sort of cash flow you can expect, based on market analysis, projection, and comparison with existing companies. Other needed information, such as personal financial history, résumés, legal documents, or pictures of your product, can be placed in *appendices*.

Use your business plan to get an idea of how much startup money is necessary and to discipline your thinking and challenge your preconceived notions before you develop your cash flow. The business plan will tell you how long it will take before you turn a profit, which in turn is linked to how long it will before you will be able to pay back investors or a bank loan—which is something that anyone supplying you with money will want to know. Even if you are planning to subsist on grants or you are not planning on investment or even starting a for-profit company, the discipline imposed by the business plan is still the first step to organizing your venture.

A business plan also gives you a realistic view of your personal financial obligations. How long can you afford to live without regular income? How are you going to afford medical insurance? When will your business begin turning a profit? How much of a profit? Will you need to reinvest your profits in the business, or can you begin living off of them? Proper planning is key to success in any venture.

A final note on business plans: Take into account realistic expected profit minus realistic costs. Many small business owners begin by underestimating start-ups and variable costs (such as electricity bills), and then underpricing their product. This effectively paints them into a corner from which it is hard to make a profit. Allow for realistic market conditions on both the supply and the demand side.

Partnering Up

You should think long and hard about the decision to go into business with a partner (or partners). Whereas other people can bring needed capital, expertise, and labor to a business, they can also be liabilities. The questions you need to ask yourself are:

☞ Will this person be a full and equal partner? In other words, are they able to carry their own weight? Make a full and fair assessment of your potential partner's personality. Going into business with someone who lacks a work ethic, or prefers giving directions to working in the trenches, can be a frustrating experience.

☞ What will they contribute to the business? For instance, a partner may bring in start-up money, facilities, or equipment. However, consider if this is enough of a reason to bring them on board. You may be able to get the same advantages in another way—for instance, renting a garage rather than working out of your partner's. Likewise, doubling skill sets does not always double productivity.

☞ Do they have any liabilities? For instance, if your prospective partner has declared bankruptcy in the past, this can hurt your collective venture's ability to get credit.

☞ Will the profits be able to sustain all the partners? Many start-up ventures do not turn profits immediately, and what little they do produce can be spread thin amongst many partners. Carefully work out the math.

Also bear in mind that going into business together can put a strain on even the best personal relationships. No matter whether it is family, friends, or strangers, keep everything very professional with written agreements regarding these investments. Get everything in writing, and be clear where obligations begin and end. "It's important to go into business with the right people," says Curtis. "If you don't—if it degrades into infighting and petty bickering—it can really go south quickly."

Incorporating. . . or Not

Think long and hard about incorporating. Starting a business often requires a fairly large—and risky—financial investment, which in turn exposes you to personal liability. Furthermore, as your business grows, so does your risk. Incorporating can help you shield yourself from this liability. However, it also has disadvantages.

To begin with, incorporating is not necessary for conducting professional transactions such as obtaining bank accounts and credit. You can do this as a sole proprietor, partnership, or simply by filing a DBA ("doing business as") statement with your local court (also known as "trading as" or an "assumed business name"). The DBA is an accounting entity that facilitates commerce and keeps your business' money separate from your own. However, the DBA does not shield you from responsibility if your business fails. It is entirely possible to ruin your credit, lose your house, and have your other assets seized in the unfortunate event of bankruptcy.

The purpose of incorporating is to shield yourself from personal financial liability. In case the worst happens, only the business' assets can be taken. However, this is not always the best solution. Check your local laws: Many states have laws that prevent a creditor from seizing a non-incorporated small business' assets in case of owner bankruptcy. If you are a corporation, however, the things you use to do business that are owned by the corporation—your office equipment, computers, restaurant refrigerators, and other essential equipment—may be seized by creditors, leaving you no way to work yourself out of debt. This is why it is imperative to consult with a lawyer.

There are other areas in which being a corporation can be an advantage, such as business insurance. Depending on your business needs, insurance can be for a variety of things: malpractice, against delivery failures or spoilage, or liability against defective products or accidents. Furthermore, it is easier to hire employees, obtain credit, and buy health insurance as an organization than as an individual. However, on the downside, corporations are subject to specific and strict laws concerning management and ownership. Again, you should consult with a knowledgeable legal expert.

Among the things you should discuss with your legal expert are the advantages and disadvantages of incorporating in your jurisdiction and which type of incorporation is best for you. The laws on liability and how much of your profit will be taken away in taxes vary widely by state and country. Generally, most small businesses owners opt for *limited liability companies* (LLCs), which gives them more control and a more flexible management structure. (Another possibility is a *limited liability partnership*, or *LLP*, which is especially useful for professionals such as doctors and lawyers.) Finally, there is the *corporation*, which is characterized by transferable ownerships shares, perpetual succession, and, of course, limited liability.

Most small businesses are sole proprietorships, partnerships, or privately-owned corporations. In the past, not many incorporated, since it was necessary to have multiple owners to start a corporation. However, this is changing, since it is now possible in many states for an individual to form a corporation. Note also that the form your business takes is usually not set in stone: A sole proprietorship or partnership can switch to become an LLC as it grows and the risks increase; furthermore, a successful LLC can raise capital by changing its structure to become a corporation and selling stock.

Legal Issues

Many other legal issues besides incorporating (or not) need to be addressed before you start your business. It is impossible to speak directly to every possible business need in this brief appendix, since regulations, licenses, and health and safety codes vary by industry and locality. A restaurant in Manhattan, for instance, has to deal not only with the usual issues such as health inspectors, and the state liquor board, but obscure regulations such as New York City's cabaret laws, which prohibit dancing without a license in a place where alcohol is sold. An asbestos-abatement company, on the other hand, has a very different set of standards it has to abide by, including federal regulations. Researching applicable laws is part of starting up any business.

Part of being a wise business owner is knowing when you need help. There is software available for things like bookkeeping, business plans, and Web site creation, but generally, consulting with a knowledgeable professional—an accountant or a lawyer (or both)—is the smartest move. One of the most common mistakes is believing that just because you have expertise in the technical aspects of a certain field, you know all about running a business in that field. Whereas some people may balk at the expense, by suggesting the best way to deal with possible problems, as well as cutting through red tape and seeing possible pitfalls that you may not even have been aware of, such professionals usually more than make up for their cost. After all, they have far more experience at this than does a first-time business owner!

Financial

Another necessary first step in starting a business is obtaining a bank account. However, having the account is not as important as what you do with it. One of the most common problems with small businesses is undercapitalization—especially in brick-and-mortar businesses that sell or make something, rather than service-based businesses. The rule of thumb is that you should have access to money equal to your first year's anticipated profits, plus start-up expenses. (Note that this is not the same as having the money on hand—see the discussion on lines of credit, below.) For instance, if your annual rent, salaries, and equipment will cost $50,000 and you expect $25,000 worth of profit in your first year, you should have access to $75,000 worth of financing.

You need to decide what sort of financing you will need. Small business loans have both advantages and disadvantages. They can provide critical start-up credit, but in order to obtain one, your personal credit will need to be good, and you will, of course, have to pay them off with interest. In general, the more you and your partners put into the business yourselves, the more credit lenders will be willing to extend to you.

Equity can come from your own personal investment, either in cash or an equity loan on your home. You may also want to consider bringing on partners—at least limited financial partners—as a way to cover start-up costs.

It is also worth considering obtaining a line of credit instead of a loan. A loan is taken out all at once, but with a line of credit, you draw on the money as you need it. This both saves you interest payments and means that you have the money you need when you need it. Taking out too large of a loan can be worse than having no money at all! It just sits there collecting interest—or, worse, is spent on something utterly un-necessary—and then is not around when you need it most.

The first five years are the hardest for any business venture; your venture has about double the usual chance of closing in this time (1 out of 6, rather than 1 out of 12). You will probably have to tighten your belt at home, as well as work long hours and keep careful track of your business expenses. Be careful with your money. Do not take unnecessary risks, play it conservatively, and always keep some capital in reserve for emergencies. The hardest part of a new business, of course, is the learning curve of figuring out what, exactly, you need to do to make a profit, and so the best advice is to have plenty of savings—or a job to provide income—while you learn the ropes.

One thing you should not do is count on venture capitalists or "angel investors," that is, businesspeople who make a living investing on other businesses in the hopes that their equity in the company will increase in value. Venture capitalists have gotten something of a reputation as indiscriminate spendthrifts due to some poor choices made during the dot-com boom of the late 1990s, but the fact is that most do not take risks on unproven products. Rather, they are attracted to young companies that have the potential to become regional or national powerhouses and give better-than-average returns. Nor are venture capitalists endless sources of money; rather, they are savvy businesspeople who are usually attracted to companies that have already experienced a measure of success. Therefore, it is better to rely on your own resources until you have proven your business will work.

Bookkeeping 101

The principles of double-entry bookkeeping have not changed much since its invention in the fifteenth century: one column records debits, and one records credits. The trick is *doing* it. As a small business owner, you need to be disciplined and meticulous at recording your finances. Thankfully, today there is software available that can do everything from tracking payables and receivables to running checks and generating reports.

Honestly ask yourself if you are the sort of person who does a good job keeping track of finances. If you are not, outsource to a bookkeeping company or hire someone to come in once or twice a week to enter invoices and generate checks for you. Also remember that if you have employees or even freelancers, you will have to file tax forms for them at the end of the year.

Another good idea is to have an accountant for your business to handle advice and taxes (federal, state, local, sales tax, etc.). In fact, consulting with a certified public accountant is a good idea in general, since they are usually aware of laws and rules that you have never even heard of.

Finally, keep your personal and business accounting separate. If your business ever gets audited, the first thing the IRS looks for is personal expenses disguised as business expenses. A good accountant can help you to know what are legitimate business expenses. Everything you take from the business account, such as payroll and reimbursement, must be recorded and classified.

Being an Employer

Know your situation regarding employees. To begin with, if you have any employees, you will need an Employer Identification Number (EIN), also sometimes called a Federal Tax Identification Number. Getting an EIN is simple: You can fill out IRS form SS-4, or complete the process online at http://www.irs.gov.

Having employees carries other responsibilities and legalities with it. To begin with, you will need to pay payroll taxes (otherwise known as "withholding") to cover income tax, unemployment insurance, Social Security, and Medicare, as well as file W-2 and W-4 forms with the government. You will also be required to pay worker's compensation insurance, and will probably also want to find medical insurance. You are also required to abide by your state's nondiscrimination laws. Most states require you to post nondiscrimination and compensation notices in a public area.

Many employers are tempted to unofficially hire workers "off the books." This can have advantages, but can also mean entering a legal gray area. (Note, however, this is different from hiring freelancers, a temp employed by another company, or having a self-employed professional such as an accountant or bookkeeper come in occasionally to provide a service.) It is one thing to hire the neighbor's teenage son on a one-time basis to help you move some boxes, but quite another to have full-time workers working on a cash-and-carry basis. Regular wages must be noted in the accounts, and gaps may be questioned in the event of an audit. If the workers are injured on the job, you are not covered by worker's comp, and are thus vulnerable to lawsuits. If the workers you hired are not legal residents, you can also be liable for civil and criminal penalties. In general, it is best to keep your employees as above-board as possible.

Building a Business

Good business practices are essential to success. First off, do not overextend yourself. Be honest about what you can do and in what time frame. Secondly, be a responsible business owner. In general, if there is a problem, it is best to explain matters honestly to your clients than to leave them without word and wondering. In the former case, there is at least the possibility of salvaging your reputation and credibility.

Most business is still built by personal contacts and word of mouth. It is for this reason that maintaining your list of contacts is an essential practice. Even if a particular contact may not be useful at a particular moment, a future opportunity may present itself—or you may be able to send someone else to them. Networking, in other words, is as important when you are the boss as when you are looking for a job yourself. As the owner of a company, having a network means getting services on better terms, knowing where to go if you need help with a particular problem, or simply being in the right place at the right time to exploit an opportunity. Join professional organizations, the local Chamber of Commerce, clubs and community organizations, and learn to play golf. And remember—never burn a bridge.

Advertising is another way to build a business. Planning an ad campaign is not as difficult as you might think: You probably already know your media market and business community. The trick is applying it. Again, go with your instincts. If you never look twice at your local weekly, other people probably do not, either. If you are in a high-tourist area, though, local tourist maps might be a good way to leverage your marketing dollar. Ask other people in your area or market who have businesses similar to your own. Depending on your focus, you might want to consider everything from AM radio or local TV networks, to national trade publications, to hiring a PR firm for an all-out blitz. By thinking about these questions, you can spend your advertising dollars most effectively.

Nor should you underestimate the power of using the Internet to build your business. It is a very powerful tool for small businesses, potentially reaching vast numbers of people for relatively little outlay of money. Launching a Web site has become the modern equivalent of hanging out your shingle. Even if you are primarily a brick-and-mortar business, a Web presence can still be an invaluable tool—your store or offices will show up on Google searches, plus customers can find directions to visit you in person. Furthermore, the Internet offers the small-business owner many useful tools. Print and design services, order fulfillment, credit card processing, and networking—both personal and in terms of linking to other sites—are all available online. Web advertising can be useful, too, either by advertising on specialty sites that appeal to your audience, or by using services such as Google AdWords.

Amateurish print ads, TV commercials, and Web sites do not speak well of your business. Good media should be well-designed, well-edited, and well-put together. It need not, however, be expensive. Shop around and, again, use your network.

Flexibility is also important. "In general, a business must adapt to changing conditions, find new customers and find new products or services that customers need when the demand for their older products or services diminishes," says James Peck, a Long Island, New York, entrepreneur. In other words, if your original plan is not working out, or if demand falls, see if you can parlay your experience, skills, and physical plant into meeting other needs. People are not the only ones who can change their path in life; organizations can, too.

A Final Word

In business, as in other areas of life, the advice of more experienced people is essential. "I think it really takes three businesses until you know what you're doing," Drew Curtis confides. "I sure didn't know what I was doing the first time." Listen to what others have to say, no matter whether it is about your Web site or your business plan. One possible solution is seeking out a mentor, someone who has previously launched a successful venture in this field. In any case, before taking any step, ask as many people as many questions as you can. Good advice is invaluable.

Further Resources

American Independent Business Alliance
http://www.amiba.net

American Small Business League
http://www.asbl.com

IRS Small Business and Self-Employed One-Stop Resource
http://www.irs.gov/businesses/small/index.html

The Riley Guide: Steps in Starting Your Own Business
http://www.rileyguide.com/steps.html

Small Business Administration
http://www.sba.gov

Appendix B

Outfitting Yourself for Career Success

As you contemplate a career shift, the first component is to assess your interests. You need to figure out what makes you tick, since there is a far greater chance that you will enjoy and succeed in a career that taps into your passions, inclinations, natural abilities, and training. If you have a general idea of what your interests are, you at least know in which direction you want to travel. You may know you want to simply switch from one sort of nursing to another, or change your life entirely and pursue a dream you have always held. In this case, you can use a specific volume of The Field Guides to Finding a New Career to discover which position to target. If you are unsure of the direction you want to take, well, then the entire scope of the series is open to you! Browse through to see what appeals to you, and see if it matches with your experience and abilities.

The next step you should take is to make a list—do it once in writing—of the skills you have used in a position of responsibility that transfer to the field you are entering. People in charge of interviewing and hiring may well understand that the skills they are looking for in a new hire are used in other fields, but you must spell it out. Most job descriptions are partly a list of skills. Map your experience into that, and very early in your contacts with a prospective employer explicitly address how you acquired your relevant skills. Pick a relatively unimportant aspect of the job to be your ready answer for where you would look forward to learning within the organization, if this seems essentially correct. When you transfer into a field, softly acknowledge a weakness while relating your readiness to learn, but never lose sight of the value you offer both in your abilities and in the freshness of your perspective.

Energy and Experience

The second component in career-switching success is energy. When Jim Fulmer was 61, he found himself forced to close his piano-repair business. However, he was able to parlay his knowledge of music, pianos, and the musical instruments industry into another job as a sales representative for a large piano manufacturer, and quickly built up a clientele of musical-instrument retailers throughout the East Coast. Fulmer's experience highlights another essential lesson for career-changers: There are plenty of opportunities out there, but jobs will not come to you—especially the career-oriented, well-paying ones. You have to seek them out.

Jim Fulmer's case also illustrates another important point: Former training and experience can be a key to success. "Anyone who has to make a career change in any stage of life has to look at what skills they have acquired but may not be aware of," he says. After all, people can more easily change into careers similar to the ones they are leaving. Training and experience also let you enter with a greater level of seniority, provided you have the other necessary qualifications. For instance, a nurse who is already experienced with administering drugs and their benefits and drawbacks, and who is also graced with the personality and charisma to work with the public, can become a pharmaceutical company sales representative.

Unlock Your Network

The next step toward unlocking the perfect job is networking. The term may be overused, but the idea is as old as civilization. More than other animals, humans need one another. With the Internet and telephone, never in history has it been easier to form (or revive) these essential links. One does not have to gird oneself and attend reunion-type events (though for many this is a fine tactic)—but keep open to opportunities to meet people who may be friendly to you in your field. Ben Franklin understood the principle well—*Poor Richard's Almanac* is something of a treatise on the importance of cultivating what Franklin called "friendships" with benefactors. So follow in the steps of the founding fathers and make friends to get ahead. Remember: helping others feels good; it's often the receiving that gets a little tricky. If you know someone particularly well-connected in your field, consider tapping one or two less important connections first so that you make the most of the important one. As you proceed, keep your strengths foremost in your mind because the glue of commerce is mutual interest.

Eighty percent of job openings are *never advertised*, and, according to the U.S. Bureau of Labor statistics, more than half of all employees landed their jobs through networking. Using your personal contacts is far more efficient and effective than trusting your résumé to the Web. On the Web, an employer needs to sort through tens of thousands—or millions—of résumés. When you direct your application to one potential employer, you are directing your inquiry to one person who already knows you. The personal touch is everything: Human beings are social animals, programmed to "read" body language; we are naturally inclined to trust those we meet in person, or who our friends and coworkers have recommended. While Web sites can be useful (for looking through help-wanted ads, for instance), expecting employers to pick you out of the slush pile is as effective as throwing your résumé into a black hole.

Do not send your résumé out just to make yourself feel like you're doing something. The proper way to go about things is to employ discipline and order, and then to apply your charm. Begin your networking efforts by making a list of people you can talk to: colleagues, coworkers, and supervisors, people you have had working relationship with, people from church, athletic teams, political organizations, or other community groups, friends, and relatives. You can expand your networking opportunities by following the suggestions in each chapter of the volumes. Your goal here is not so much to land a job as to expand your possibilities and knowledge: Though the people on your list may not be in the position to help you themselves, they might know someone who is. Meeting with them might also help you understand traits that matter and skills that are valued in the field in which you are interested. Even if the person is a potential employer, it is best to phrase your request as if you were seeking information: "You might not be able to help me, but do you know someone I could talk to who could tell me more about what it is like to work in this field?" Being hungry gives one impression, being desperate quite another.

Keep in mind that networking is a two-way street. If you meet someone who has an opening that is not right for you, but you could recommend someone else, you have just added to your list two people who will be favorably disposed toward you in the future. Also, bear in mind that *you* can help people in *your* old field, thus adding to your own contacts list.

Networking is especially important to the self-employed or those who start their own businesses. Many people in this situation begin because they either recognize a potential market in a field that they are familiar with, or because full-time employment in this industry is no longer a possibility. Already being well-established in a field can help, but so can asking connections for potential work and generally making it known that you are ready, willing, and able to work. Working your professional connections, in many cases, is the *only* way to establish yourself. A free-lancer's network, in many cases, is like a spider's web. The spider casts out many strands, since he or she never knows which one might land the next meal.

Dial-Up Help

In general, it is better to call contacts directly than to e-mail them. E-mails are easy for busy people to ignore or overlook, even if they do not mean to. Explain your situation as briefly as possible (see the discussion of the "elevator speech"), and ask if you could meet briefly, either at their office or at a neutral place such as a café. (Be sure that you pay the bill in such a situation—it is a way of showing you appreciate their time and effort.) If you get someone's voicemail, give your "elevator speech" and then say you will call back in a few days to follow up—and then do so. If you reach your contact directly and they are too busy to speak or meet with you, make a definite appointment to call back at a later date. Be persistent, but not annoying.

Once you have arranged a meeting, prep yourself. Look at industry publications both in print and online, as well as news reports (here, GoogleNews, which lets you search through online news reports, can be very handy). Having up-to-date information on industry trends shows that you are dedicated, knowledgeable, and focused. Having specific questions on employers and requests for suggestions will set you apart from the rest of the job-hunting pack. Knowing the score—for instance, asking about the value of one sort of certification instead of another— pegs you as an "insider," rather than a dilettante, someone whose name is worth remembering and passing along to a potential employer.

Finally, set the right mood. Here, a little self-hypnosis goes a long way: Look at yourself in the mirror, and tell yourself that you are an enthusiastic, committed professional. Mood affects confidence and per-formance. Discipline your mind so you keep your perspective and self-respect. Nobody wants to hire someone who comes across as insincere, tells a sob story, or is still in the doldrums of having lost their previous job. At the end of any networking meeting, ask for someone else who might be able to help you in your journey to finding a position in this field, either with information or a potential job opening.

Get a Lift

When you meet with a contact in person (as well as when you run into anyone by chance who may be able to help you), you need an "elevator speech" (so-named because it should be short enough to be delivered during an elevator ride from a ground level to a high floor). This is a summary in which, in less than two minutes, you give them a clear impression of who you are, where you come from, your experience and goals, and why you are on the path you are on. The motto above Plato's Academy holds true: Know Thyself (this is where our Career Compasses and guides will help you). A long and rambling "elevator story" will get you nowhere. Furthermore, be positive: Neither a sad-sack story nor a tirade explaining how everything that went wrong in your old job is someone else's fault will get you anywhere. However, an honest explanation of a less-than-fortunate circumstance, such as a decline in business forcing an office closure, needing to change residence to a place where you are not qualified to work in order to further your spouse's career, or needing to work fewer hours in order to care for an ailing family member, is only honest.

An elevator speech should show 1) you know the business involved; 2) you know the company; 3) you are qualified (here, try to relate your education and work experience to the new situation); and 4) you are goal-oriented, dependable, and hardworking. Striking a balance is important; you want to sound eager, but not overeager. You also want to show a steady work experience, but not that you have been so narrowly focused that you cannot adjust. Most important is emphasizing what you can do for the company. You will be surprised how much information you can include in two minutes. Practice this speech in front of a mirror until you have the key points down perfectly. It should sound natural, and you should come across as friendly, confident, and assertive. Finally, remember eye contact! Good eye contact needs to be part of your presentation, as well as your everyday approach when meeting potential employers and leads.

Get Your Résumé Ready

Everyone knows what a résumé is, but how many of us have really thought about how to put one together? Perhaps no single part of the job search is subject to more anxiety—or myths and misunderstandings—than this 8 ½-by-11-inch sheet of paper.

On the one hand, it is perfectly all right for someone—especially in certain careers, such as academia—to have a résumé that is more than one page. On the other hand, you do not need to tell a future employer *everything*. Trim things down to the most relevant; for a 40-year-old to mention an internship from two decades ago is superfluous. Likewise, do not include irrelevant jobs, lest you seem like a professional career-changer.

Tailor your descriptions of your former employment to the particular position you are seeking. This is not to say you should lie, but do make your experience more appealing. If the job you're looking for involves supervising other people, say if you have done this in the past; if it involves specific knowledge or capabilities, mention that you possess these qualities. In general, try to make your past experience seem similar to what you are seeking.

The standard advice is to put your Job Objective at the heading of the résumé. An alternative to this is a Professional Summary, which some recruiters and employers prefer. The difference is that a Job Objective mentions the position you are seeking, whereas a Professional Summary mentions your background (e.g. "Objective: To find a position as a sales representative in agribusiness machinery" versus "Experienced sales representative; strengths include background in agribusiness, as well as building team dynamics and market expansion"). Of course, it is easy to come up with two or three versions of the same document for different audiences.

The body of the résumé of an experienced worker varies a lot more than it does at the beginning of your career. You need not put your education or your job experience first; rather, your résumé should emphasize your strengths. If you have a master's degree in a related field, that might want to go before your unrelated job experience. Conversely, if too much education will harm you, you might want to bury that under the section on professional presentations you have given that show how good you are at communicating. If you are currently enrolled in a course or other professional development, be sure to note this (as well as your date of expected graduation). A résumé is a study of blurs, highlights, and jewels. You blur everything you must in order to fit the description of your experience to the job posting. You highlight what is relevant from each and any of your positions worth mentioning. The jewels are the little headers and such—craft them, since they are what is seen first.

You may also want to include professional organizations, work-related achievements, and special abilities, such as your fluency in a foreign language. Also mention your computer software qualifications and capabilities, especially if you are looking for work in a technological field or if you are an older job-seeker who might be perceived as behind the technology curve. Including your interests or family information might or might not be a good idea—no one really cares about your bridge club, and in fact they might worry that your marathon training might take away from your work commitments, but, on the other hand, mentioning your golf handicap or three children might be a good idea if your potential employer is an avid golfer or is a family woman herself.

You can either include your references or simply note, "References available upon request." However, be sure to ask your references' permission to use their names and alert them to the fact that they may be contacted before you include them on your résumé! Be sure to include name, organization, phone number, and e-mail address for each contact.

Today, word processors make it easy to format your résumé. However, beware of prepackaged résumé "wizards"—they do not make you stand out in the crowd. Feel free to strike out on your own, but remember the most important thing in formatting a résumé is consistency. Unless you have a background in typography, do not get too fancy. Finally, be sure to have someone (or several people!) read your résumé over for you.

For more information on résumé writing, check out Web sites such as http://www.résumé.monster.com.

Craft Your Cover Letter

It is appropriate to include a cover letter with your résumé. A cover letter lets you convey extra information about yourself that does not fit or is not always appropriate in your résumé, such as why you are no longer working in your original field of employment. You can and should also mention the name of anyone who referred you to the job. You can go into some detail about the reason you are a great match, given the job description. Also address any questions that might be raised in the potential employer's mind (for instance, a gap in employment). Do not, however, ramble on. Your cover letter should stay focused on your goal: To offer a strong, positive impression of yourself and persuade the hiring manager that you are worth an interview. Your cover letter gives you a chance to stand out from the other applicants and sell yourself. In fact, according to a CareerBuilder. com survey, 23 percent of hiring managers say a candidate's ability to relate his or her experience to the job at hand is a top hiring consideration.

Even if you are not a great writer, you can still craft a positive yet concise cover letter in three paragraphs: An introduction containing the specifics of the job you are applying for; a summary of why you are a good fit for the position and what you can do for the company; and a closing with a request for an interview, contact information, and thanks. Remember to vary the structure and tone of your cover letter—do not begin every sentence with "I."

Ace Your Interview

In truth, your interview begins well before you arrive. Be sure to have read up well on the company and its industry. Use Web sites and magazines—http://www.hoovers.com offers free basic business information, and trade magazines deliver both information and a feel for the industries they cover. Also, do not neglect talking to people in your circle who might know about trends in the field. Leave enough time to digest the information so that you can give some independent thought to the company's history and prospects. You don't need to be an expert when you arrive to be interviewed; but you should be comfortable. The most important element of all is to be poised and relaxed during the interview itself. Preparation and practice can help a lot.

Be sure to develop well-thought-through answers to the following, typical interview openers and standard questions.

☞ Tell me about yourself. (Do not complain about how unsatisfied you were in your former career, but give a brief summary of your applicable background and interest in the particular job area.) If there is a basis to it, emphasize how much you love to work and how you are a team player.

☞ Why do you want this job? (Speak from the brain, and the heart—of course you want the money, but say a little here about what you find interesting about the field and the company's role in it.)

☞ What makes you a good hire? (Remember here to connect the company's needs and your skill set. Ultimately, your selling points probably come down to one thing: you will make your employer money. You want the prospective hirer to see that your skills are valuable not to the world in general but to this specific company's bottom line. What can you do for them?)

☞ What led you to leave your last job? (If you were fired, still try to say something positive, such as, "The business went through a challenging time, and some of the junior marketing people were let go.")

Practice answering these and other questions, and try to be genuinely positive about yourself, and patient with the process. Be secure but not cocky; don't be shy about forcing the focus now and then on positive contributions you have made in your working life—just be specific. As with the elevator speech, practice in front of the mirror.

A couple pleasantries are as natural a way as any to start the actual interview, but observe the interviewer closely for any cues to fall silent and formally begin. Answer directly; when in doubt, finish your phrase and look to the interviewer. Without taking command, you can always ask, "Is there more you would like to know?" Your attentiveness will convey respect. Let your personality show too—a positive attitude and a grounded sense of your abilities will go a long way to getting you considered. During the interview, keep your cell phone off and do not look at your watch. Toward the end of your meeting, you may be asked whether you have any questions. It is a good idea to have one or two in mind. A few examples follow:

☞ "What makes your company special in the field?"

☞ "What do you consider the hardest part of this position?"

☞ "Where are your greatest opportunities for growth?"

☞ "Do you know when you might need anything further from me?"

Leave discussion of terms for future conversations. Make a cordial, smooth exit.

Remember to Follow Up

Send a thank-you note. Employers surveyed by CareerBuilder.com in 2005 said it matters. About 15 percent said they would not hire someone who did not follow up with a thanks. And almost 33 percent would think less of a candidate. The form of the note does not much matter—if you know a manager's preference, use it. Otherwise, just be sure to follow up.

Winning an Offer

A job offer can feel like the culmination of a long and difficult struggle. So naturally, when you hear them, you may be tempted to jump at the offer. Don't. Once an employer wants you, he or she will usually give you a chance to consider the offer. This is the time to discuss terms of employment, such as vacation, overtime, and benefits. A little effort now can be well worth it in the future. Be sure to do a check of prevailing salaries for your field and area before signing on. Web sites for this include Payscale.com, Salary.com, and Salaryexpert.com. If you are thinking about asking for better or different terms from what the prospective employer offered, rest assured—that's how business gets done; and it may just burnish the positive impression you have already made.

Index

A

accountant, 25–33
    age group landmarks, 32–33
    career compasses, 25
    certification, 26, 32
    earnings, 28
    education/training, 27–28
    employment outlook, 25–26
    essential gear, 26, 32
    job description, 25–28
    related work experience, 28
    resources, 31, 33
    testimonial, 30–31
    transition expedition, 29–32
    types of, xii, 26–27
    work environments, 27
age group landmarks
    accountant, 32–33
    auditor, 42
    bookkeeper, 80
    brand manager, 61–62
    claims adjuster, 69–71
    financial analyst, 10–11
    insurance underwriter, 90
    loan officer, 97–98
    personal financial advisor, 22
    stockbroker, 51
auditor, xii, 35–43
    age group landmarks, 42
    career compasses, 35
    certification, 36
    education/training, 38, 41–42
    employment outlook, 36
    essential gear, 36, 37
    job description, 35–37
    related work experience, 39–40
    resources, 42–43
    skills/qualifications, 37
    testimonial, 40–41
    transition expedition, 39–42
    work environments, 39

B

bookkeeper, xii, 74–81
    age group landmarks, 80
    career compasses, 74
    certification, 76, 79
    education/training, 76
    employment outlook, 75
    essential gear, 75, 80
    job description, 74–76
    related work experience, 76
    resources, 81
    skills/qualifications, 75, 77
    testimonial, 78–79
    transition expedition, 77–79
brand manager, 55–62
    age group landmarks, 61–62
    career compasses, 55
    certification, 57
    education/training, 56, 57, 58
    essential gear, 56, 57
    job description, 55–57
    related work experience, 58–59
    resources, 62
    skills/qualifications, 56–57
    testimonial, 60–61
    transition expedition, 59–60
business, starting own, 103–113
    bookkeeping for, 109–110
    building, 111–112
    employer in, being, 110–111
    financial issues in, 108–109
    incorporation of, 106–107
    legal issues in, 107–108
    partnership in, 105–106
    plan, 103–105

resources for, 113

testimonial on, 117–118

C

careers

new, vii–viii

successful, 117–126

career compasses

accountant, 25

auditor, 35

bookkeeper, 74

brand manager, 55

claims adjuster, 64

financial analyst, 2

insurance underwriter, 83

loan officer, 92

personal financial advisor, 13

stockbroker, 45

certification/registration, xiv

accountant, 26, 32

auditor, 36

bookkeeper, 76, 79

brand manager, 57

financial analyst, 3, 8, 9, 10

insurance underwriter, 85–86

loan officer, 93, 99

personal financial advisor, 15, 21

claims adjuster, xiii–xiv, 64–72

age group landmarks, 69–71

career compasses, 64

earnings, 68

education/training, 66, 67

employment outlook, 67

essential gear, 65, 66, 69

job description, 64–67

related work experience, 64, 67

resources, 72–73

skills/qualifications, 67

testimonial, 71–72

transition expedition, 68–69

CPE (Certified Fraud Examiners), 32

E

earnings

accountant, 28

claims adjuster, 68

loan officer, 94

personal financial advisor, 14–15, 20

stockbroker, 47

education/training, xiv. *See also* certification/
registration

accountant, 27–28

auditor, 38, 41–42

bookkeeper, 76

brand manager, 56, 57, 58

claims adjuster, 66, 67

financial analyst, 4–5, 10

insurance underwriter, 85–86, 89

loan officer, 94, 95, 97

personal financial advisor, 15, 21

stockbroker, 46, 49

elevator speech, 121

employer, starting own business as, 110–111

employment outlook

accountant, 25–26

auditor, 36

bookkeeper, 75

claims adjuster, 67

financial analyst, 4

personal financial advisor, 16

equity, business and, 108

essential gear

accountant, 26, 32

auditor, 36, 37

bookkeeper, 75, 80

brand manager, 56, 57

claims adjuster, 65, 66, 69

financial analyst, 3, 4

insurance underwriter, 84, 85

loan officer, 93, 94

personal financial advisor, 14, 15, 21

stockbroker, 46, 47

F

fifties, age group

accountants in, 33

auditors in, 42

bookkeepers in, 80

brand managers in, 62

claims adjusters in, 70

financial analysts in, 11

insurance underwriters in, 90

loan officers in, 98

personal financial advisors in, 22

stockbrokers in, 51

finance, business and, 108–109

financial analyst, xii, xiii, 2–10

age group landmarks, 10–11

career compasses, 2

certification, 3, 8, 9, 10

education/training, 4–5, 10

employment outlook, 4

essential gear, 3, 4

job description, 2–6

related work experience, 5, 10

resources, 11

skills/qualifications, 6–7

testimonial, 8–9

transition expedition, 7–10

work environments, 7

follow up, interview, 126

forensic accountant, 27

I

incorporation, 106–107

insurance underwriter, xiii, 83–90

age group landmarks, 90

career compasses, 83

certification/registration, 85–86

education/training, 85–86, 89

essential gear, 84, 85

job description, 83–86

related work experience, 86

resources, 90

skills/qualifications, 85, 86

testimonial, 88–89

transition expedition, 87–89

interview, 124–126

J

jobs

changing, vii, viii

offer, 126

U. S. loss of, vii

job descriptions

accountant, 25–28

auditor, 35–37

bookkeeper, 74–76

brand manager, 55–57

claims adjuster, 64–67

financial analyst, 2–6

insurance underwriter, 83–86

loan officer, 92–94

personal financial advisor, 13–17

stockbroker, 45–48

L

legal issues, business, 107–108

licensing, stockbroker, 46–47, 50, 51

loan officer, xiii, 92–99

age group landmarks, 97–98

career compasses, 92

certification, 93, 99

earnings, 94

education/training, 94, 95, 97

essential gear, 93, 94

job description, 92–94

resources, 99

skills/qualifications, 95–96

testimonial, 98–99

transition expedition, 96–97

M

microbusinesses, 103

N

networking, 118–120

P

partners, business, 105–106

personal financial advisor, xi, xiii, xiv, 13–23

age group landmarks, 22

career compasses, 13

certification, 15, 21

earnings, 14–15, 20

education/training, 15, 21

employment outlook, 16

essential gear, 14, 15, 21

job description, 13–17

related work experience, 17–18

resources, 22–23

skills/qualifications, 19

testimonial, 18–19

transition expedition, 20–21

work environments, 14

R

registration. *See* certification/registration

related work experience

accountant, 28

auditor, 39–40

bookkeeper, 76

brand manager, 58–59

claims adjuster, 64, 67

financial analyst, 5, 10

insurance underwriter, 86

personal financial advisor, 17–18

stockbroker, 48–49

resources

accountant, 31, 33

auditor, 42–43

bookkeeper, 81

brand manager, 62

business, starting own, 113

claims adjuster, 72–73

financial analyst, 11

insurance underwriter, 90

loan officer, 99

personal financial advisor, 22–23

stockbroker, 51–52

résumé, 122–124

S

sixties plus, age group

accountants in, 33

auditors in, 42

bookkeepers in, 80

brand managers in, 62

claims adjusters in, 71

financial analysts in, 11

insurance underwriters in, 90

loan officers in, 98

personal financial advisors in, 22

stockbrokers in, 51

skills/qualifications

auditor, 37

bookkeeper, 75, 77

brand manager, 56–57

claims adjuster, 67

financial analyst, 6–7

insurance underwriter, 85, 86

loan officer, 95–96

personal financial advisor, 19

stockbroker, 48, 50

telephone, 120–121

Small Business Administration, 113

stockbroker, 45–53

age group landmarks, 51

career compasses, 45

earnings, 47
education/training, 46, 49
essential gear, 46, 47
job description, 45–48
licensing, 46–47, 50, 51
related work experience, 48–49
resources, 51–52
skills/qualifications, 48, 50
testimonial, 52–53
transition expedition, 50–51
success, career, 117–127

T

telephone skills, 120–121
testimonials
accountant, 30–31
auditor, 40–41
bookkeeper, 78–79
brand manager, 60–61
business, starting own, 117–118
claims adjuster, 71–72
financial analyst, 8–9
insurance underwriter, 88–89
loan officer, 98–99
personal financial advisor, 18–19
stockbroker, 52–53
thirties/forties, age group
accountants in, 32
auditors in, 42
bookkeepers in, 80
brand managers in, 61–62
claims adjusters in, 69–70
financial analysts in, 10–11

insurance underwriters in, 90
loan officers in, 97
personal financial advisors in, 22
stockbrokers in, 51
transition expedition
accountant, 29–32
auditor, 39–42
bookkeeper, 77–79
brand manager, 59–60
claims adjuster, 68–69
financial analyst, 7–10
insurance underwriter, 87–89
loan officer, 96–97
personal financial advisor, 20–21
stockbroker, 50–51
twenties, age group
accountants in, 32
auditors in, 42
bookkeepers in, 80
brand managers in, 61
claims adjusters in, 69
financial analysts in, 10
insurance underwriters in, 90
loan officers in, 97
personal financial advisors in, 22
stockbrokers in, 51

W

work environments
accountant, 27
auditor, 39
financial analyst, 7
personal financial advisor, 14